DO-IT-YOURSELF BRAIN SURGERY!

101 Revolutionary New Brain Science Strategies

YOU Can Implant in Your Brain RIGHT NOW to

Skyrocket Your Achievements,

Productivity, Performance Levels and Generate

Outrageous Income Ideas!

©2010 by Doug Bench

Editing by *Purposed by Design Communications:*
Georgina Chong-You
Gainesville, Florida

Cover Design by Amanda Myer

For more information or to purchase additional copies,
contact:

The Brain Training Academy

P O Box G   McIntosh, FL 32664

Phone 888 348-2724

Email Doug@brainapples.com

ISBN: 978-1-60458-442-4

Printed in the United States.

The Brain Apples Blueprint

Presents

DO-IT-YOURSELF BRAIN SURGERY!

101 Revolutionary New Brain Science Strategies

YOU Can Implant in Your Brain **RIGHT NOW** to

Skyrocket Your Achievements,

Productivity, Performance Levels and Generate

Outrageous Income Ideas!

Doug Bench, MS JD AAAS

2010

Books, CD Systems and Reports by Doug Bench, MS JD AAAS:

The Brain Training Academy presents:

Revolutionize Your Brain! Revolutionary new brain science discoveries and the 16 *Brain Apples* techniques you can develop for **permanent** self-motivation and a lifetime of greater achievements.

***Do-it-Yourself Brain Surgery* 101** revolutionary new brain science strategies you can implant in your brain RIGHT NOW to skyrocket your achievements, productivity and performance levels!

Science on the Sidelines How to use new brain science discoveries to always coach an undefeated team...no matter what the final score!

Don't You Dare Diet! The Neuroscience of Weight Control Change your thoughts to change your brain and control your weight!

The Neuroscience of Prayer Can prayer create physiological changes in your brain and your life?

Staying Brain Sharp! How to use brain science discoveries to maintain and even improve your brain's cognition, no matter what your age!

The Neuroscience of Leadership and Change It's all in **their** head! Why is it so darn hard to change and what you can do about it! What the new brain research tells us!

Check out our Websites:

www.scienceforsuccess.com

www.brainapples.com

www.thebraintrainingblog.com

www.thebraintrainingacademy.com

www.ceuseminarsecrets.com

www.floridahardhat.com

www.yourweddingvows.com

www.howtofindyourfamilytree.com

www.ride-n-tote.com

www.manelybling.com

Do-it-Yourself Brain Surgery!

Table of Contents

Introduction

About nine years ago, I developed a keen interest in the human brain. In the beginning, it was specifically MY brain I was interested in.

My brother, sister and I had just lost our mother at age 90, after she struggled tragically for six years with that horrific disease called Alzheimer's.

When you focus on something for so long, like Alzheimer's disease, you start to notice things about yourself. And I was scared. Even though I was just in my mid-fifties then, I thought for sure I was getting Alzheimer's too because of the things I saw myself doing, such as misplacing my keys or glasses, or entering a room and forgetting why I was there.

Before my mother's battle, I wouldn't have thought twice about any of those things. But now, it's all I think about. Is it hereditary? Will I be able to stop it? I'm 54 years old, when can I expect it to happen? Are my little "senior moments" the beginning of something much more serious? With all of my questions, I had to find out more about what Alzheimer's really was.

So, I started reading everything I could get my hands on that referred to the brain and Alzheimer's. I first read Dr Pierce Howard's book, *The Owner's Manual for the Brain* (written in 1993), and I have never stopped reading.

With each new thing I read, I became more and more intrigued and interested in what I was finding. And I was reading it all at exactly the right time!

In the last 10-12 years, there has been an explosion of research producing revolutionary findings about the workings of the human brain. With the development of highly sophisticated brain-imagery tools in the mid-90s, scientists were able to see functions of the brain that they were never able to see before! They were now able to tell us astounding things about how the brain works that, as Dr. Richard Restak says in his 2003 book, *The New Brain*, was until recently "the stuff of science fiction".

All of a sudden, I was seeing, hearing, and reading about phenomenal discoveries, such as **DSPs (Dendrite Spine Protuberances), the Amygdala (an almond-shaped neural structure in the anterior part of the temporal lobe of the cerebrum that just about runs everything!), Neuroplasticity -- the greatest brain research discovery ever, and the RAS (Reticular Activating System-a complex neural network in the central core of the brainstem)**-all of which have an astounding effect on the performance of the brain.

The more I read, the more I realized that this information could have a profound impact on how well the brain works and how much you could achieve if you could learn it all and then apply it in your life!

I wrote down everything important that I read about Alzheimer's and the brain and when my notes exceeded 450 pages, I realized I had to put this information into a book (or two!), and *The Brain Training Academy* was born.

I've put together 101 facts, ideas, skills, and strategies, that are based on cutting-edge brain research and you can use them right now to advance your achievements, your productivity and your performance levels.

You need this information immediately! So here are the 101 science-based ideas and strategies that – if implanted into your brain – will help you to help yourself to improve your brain. They aren't some hocus-pocus motivational clichés, just the scientific facts. Do-it-yourself brain surgery! Non-Invasive!

I should also point out, that many of these science-based strategies will make more sense to you when you read our second book, *Revolutionize Your Brain!* This book goes into great detail about the brain, the recent revolutionary research discoveries, and our *16 Brain Apples Techniques for Permanent Change* for your brain.

So put on your surgical gown and get scrubbed up! We're about to operate on your brain!

Doug Bench

Do-it-Yourself Brain Surgery!

101 Bite-Size Brain APPLES Implants

What is a brain apple? It is a fact, skill, technique, strategy or information based on recent revolutionary brain-research discoveries that, when implanted (learned, absorbed and applied) in your brain, will help your **A**chievements, **P**roductivity, and **P**erformance **L**evels **E**levate **S**ubstantially!

Let's go to the operating room!

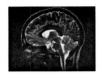

Brain Apples Implant #1: You are what you think.

When I first started reading all of the phenomenal brain research findings, one of the first and most important discoveries I made about the brain is that permanent changes in behavior and actions require time. Changes in the brain don't occur quickly.

> **To be permanently motivated to achieve at higher levels, it has to come from within you, and it takes time!**

As a motivational speaker, I learned that I couldn't motivate you to create permanent changes in your brain and, therefore, in your behavior with a one-hour speech. Long-term change takes time and must come from within *you*, not from my extrinsic ramblings of motivational cliché after cliché. Those motivational clichés used by so many speakers who claim to be gurus on success really have little permanent impact on your behavior and actions. Most of their crap is probably dissipated from your short-term memory without even going into your long-term memory and is vaporized before you get out to your car in the parking lot!

Therefore, I try my best to avoid using motivational clichés. However, I will use just one: "You are what you think." Most of us have heard that statement many times before, haven't we? But this cliché is different; it's actually a scientific fact! You are indeed what you think.

When you think at the conscious level, there are only two things you can do with your thoughts:

1. Initiate a thought of your own by coming up with an original, internally-created thought.

2. Respond with a thought in reaction to an external stimulus, something that comes to you through one of your senses at the conscious level.

Those are the only two things you can do. What's most important to understand is that you control both of these possibilities; you control any original thought you generate because you willfully create the neurons that fire it. You also control the thoughts you use to respond to external stimuli.

If your spouse comes home from the office, slams down her briefcase, and says to you, "I am so angry at Mr. Smith," you probably should calmly get up from the table and go out to the garage, looking for Mr. Smith. He must be in the car. He must have come home with her if she's so angry NOW!

Of course he's not there. Your spouse alone is controlling and creating that anger thought, not Mr. Smith.

Control these two processes of thinking and you can control your life. The problem is that we don't do the majority of our thinking at the conscious level. We do the vast majority of our thinking at the **non-conscious level.**

The brain has six levels, or areas, of thinking. One is the conscious level. As I said earlier, you control the two types of thoughts you can fire at the conscious level. But what about the non-conscious level? Those thoughts are habits—automated, reflexive thoughts that fire in a habitual way.

> *You totally control any original thought you generate*

But here's the good news: One of the biggest scientific discoveries of all time about the brain is that your non-conscious actions are based on the most dominant thoughts you fire, the dominant thoughts that you think about at your conscious level. The thoughts in the non-conscious part of your brain automatically control almost all your actions. And those thoughts are based on the dominant thoughts you have over and over again at the conscious level.

Almost all your thinking as an adult is done by habit at the non-conscious level. A **habit** is formed by firing the same DSP patterns, the same neuron patterns, over and over. In other words, habit is simply the result of thinking in a habitual way. Pretty soon that thinking becomes a habit and before long it controls your thinking. This will result in your actions occurring nearly automatically, outside your conscious control.

If your conscious brain has a particular dominant thought, your non-conscious level takes it as a

8

directive to generate thoughts, solutions and actions for those dominant thoughts.

My good friend, Dr. Jill Ammon Wexler, is an expert on the human brain. (see her website at www.quantum-self.com) Dr. Jill likes to tell the story of the teacher who comes into her elementary-school classroom and announces to her students the results of a scientific study that indicates that blue-eyed children are more intelligent and perform at higher levels in academic skills than green or brown-eyed children. She gave them an explanation for that and then each day reminded her students of that study. Over the next 90 days, the blue-eyed students in her classroom started to perform at much higher levels, and the brown and green-eyed children started performing at lower levels.

After this 90-day period, the teacher came into the classroom with a very sad look and announced to the students that she had to apologize; she had made a terrible mistake. The study actually showed the opposite: that the brown and green-eyed children did better and were smarter than the blue-eyed children. And she reminded her students of this over the next days and weeks.

The result? The green and brown-eyed children started doing better in class. The blue-eyed children started doing worse in class.

Conclusion: If you believe you are smart, you will THINK and ACT smart. If you believe you are creative, you will ACT creatively. If you believe

you are a success, you will ACT successfully. You are as you think; you act as you think.

As we've said, when you think at the conscious level, there are only two things you can do: You can create an original thought that affirms that you are smart and believes that you perform at high levels, or respond to external stimuli with a negative thought.

> **Successful people ACT successfully.**

The students in this class responded to the external stimuli, or information, that said that either blue-eyed children are smart or green and brown-eyed children are smart. If those conscious thoughts dominate your thinking, they will influence your non-conscious thoughts, which are at least 5/6 of your thinking. This 5/6 controls your behavior or actions most of the time. Therefore, you are as you think, and if you think you are a particular way, you will act that way. Notice I said, "Act that way." That's what makes you successful.

So what should you do to control your conscious thoughts?

For the next month, at least 5 days a week, take 12 minutes out of each day to learn to be a thinker and learn to observe how you think. In other words, **practice thinking.** Go to a quiet place where you won't be disturbed and practice thinking. Some of these 5 days should be at work, and some should be on the weekends or when you're not working. For just 12 minutes each day, attempt to step outside of yourself, and observe yourself thinking, your thoughts, and how one thought leads to another.

Like watching yourself think on a TV screen, observe whether you're having an original thought or a response to external stimuli. Even make notes on how this thought led to that thought and that thought led to another thought. Become an expert on observing how you think. Become a professional, knowledgeable thinker about the process of thinking. If you want to change your brain and your life, you must observe and acknowledge the process by which you do your thinking. Become an expert on how and what you think, because you act as you think, and as you act, so you shall be.

> **Your actions reflect what you think, and good thinking is a discipline.**

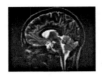

Brain Apples Implant #2: What are you telling your brain?

I found the following *Implant* to be personally disturbing. You and I have in our lives, exactly what we've been telling ourselves (with our thoughts) that we want in our lives. Each of our physical worlds reflects all the thinking we've been doing or the thinking that we've not been doing.

> **If you want to change your actions, the first step is to observe the mental images that you've been creating.**

Thoughts are mental pictures and images that may not always be in focus. You have in your life today exactly what those mental images have been telling you. So if the results aren't what you would like, you absolutely must give guidance to your conscious brain so it will then transfer that guidance over to your much more powerful non-conscious brain to reflect what you really want in your life.

If you want to change your thoughts and change your life, you've got to observe the mental images that you've been sending through your brain!

Whatever those images and thoughts have been is exactly what you have in your life now.

If you want to change your life and achieve at higher levels, you must take full responsibility for your own thoughts. Because it is *your* thoughts that have created exactly what you have in your life today. You can't change your life by *trying* to change your life. You must change your thoughts. ***Responsibility ALWAYS trumps entitlement!***

What directions are you sending to your brain?

Positive or negative?

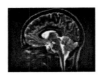

Brain Apples Implant #3: ***Your conscious thoughts direct the performance of your non-conscious brain.***

Your non-conscious brain's performance is always 80-800 times better than the performance you can generate from your conscious brain alone. Impulses (thoughts) that travel through your non-conscious levels of thought move up to 800 times faster than the thoughts you create and generate at the conscious level. The thoughts of your non-conscious brain, which is about 83% of your thinking, are all created automatically and control nearly all of your actions and behavior. **Dominant thoughts from your conscious thinking are taken as an order by your non-conscious** to come up with solutions, directions or behavior for that thought or thoughts. Therefore, if somehow you can direct your conscious thoughts toward your non-conscious brain, you can automatically perform at much higher levels.

View the following web site:

www.scienceforsuccess.com/picpuzz.htm

On this web page, you'll see a pattern of images. Look at them closely and try to find something different. You will to be able to see how your non-conscious brain can perform duties and reach for goals much quicker and better once you give it directions from your conscious level. Your non-conscious will follow the directions exactly, quickly, and explicitly. Simply observe the drawing to see if there is anything different from the other parts of that drawing; look for features that are unusual or out of the ordinary. There might be more than one thing that's different.

>>>Stop now and do this exercise.

Did you find the differences? If you look very carefully, you'll see that there are one or two plus signs (+) in the drawing where the vertical line is a different color than the rest. Most of them are <u>red</u> vertically, but one or two of them are <u>green</u>. I hope you noticed that the <u>blue</u> square is not sitting like the rest; it's sitting in such a way to make it a diamond shape.

That wasn't too tough, was it? Now I want you to solicit the help of **two** of your family members or friends. You're about to see a phenomenal thing. Ask one friend to give instructions to their non-conscious brain when they look at this picture. Don't ask that of your other friend. Time them. Bring in your first friend and don't let the second friend see the picture yet. Say to your first friend, "Take a look at this drawing and let me know, by raising your hand, when you find something different or unusual about it." Keep track of the time it takes your friend to find one or more of the things that are different.

Next, bring in friend number two, and tell them that they're looking at the drawing for something different or unusual, but you will give them some guidance, a hint, that they can pass on to their non-conscious brain via their conscious brain. Let them know that they're looking for a vertical stripe on the plus signs that's a different color, or they're looking for a square that is unusual or different from the other blue squares in the drawing. Then, start your watch to see how long it takes your second friend to raise his/her hand.

What you'll notice, of course, is that your second friend and you too, can very quickly and easily find the differences in the picture once you have some **instruction** about what you're looking for. From their conscious level, your friend sent some direction or guidance to their non-conscious level that told the non-conscious what they were looking for, and then their non-conscious brain went about finding it. The person who knew what they were looking for consciously, used their non-conscious brain to find those differences by scanning the drawing almost instantly; much more quickly than you or your first friend could by using just your conscious level of thought. Your non-conscious brain didn't know what it was looking for when you and your friend first looked at that picture. Therefore, it took some time to find the differences.

So, just like setting goals, the more specific the direction, the more focused your goals, the better you will perform. It's a simple scientific fact. If you give specific directions to your non-conscious brain via your conscious thoughts, you'll get to your goals quicker, faster, better, and with a higher level of performance.

The final point here is this: If your thoughts control who you are, what you have in your life, and how you think and believe, that is how you will act, and how you act is who you are and what you can achieve.

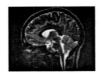

Brain Apples Implant #4: All meaningful change within your brain starts as a falsehood.

Every meaningful change you make in your life, every action you take, every performance you give, starts as a falsehood, an imagination or visualization and then comes up to your conscious level where it can be applied in your actions. That's right, **it starts as a lie.**

This is wonderful news, because we often beat ourselves up and say, "I can't do that, I don't know how. I don't believe that's possible." Great! **You don't have to *believe* you can do it. You don't need to *think* you can succeed.** Every single action, change, goal and achievement starts as an imagination or visualization, a falsehood that is created in your brain. These never start out as real! But the false thoughts will help you achieve what becomes real!

> *Turn on your VCR:*
> *Visualization Creates*
> *Reality.*

I call these "future memories"—creating memories that you have not yet experienced by creating them first as thoughts or "imaginehoods" in your brain. Therefore, it's important to develop and practice your imagination and visualization skills.

Every single idea or concept starts as unreal before it becomes real. With that knowledge, I could never understand how parents could ever discourage their children from blossoming their imaginative skills. Instead, creativity should be thoroughly encouraged.

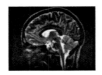

Brain Apples Implant #5: You don't always need a PMA.

Scientifically, you don't always need a positive mental attitude or positive feelings to be a high achiever. So stop beating yourself up if you can't always create a positive attitude.

I live in Central Florida. In 2004, we had four hurricanes, one right after another, starting in late August. Three of those hurricanes hit our house. The fourth one hit my son's house in Tallahassee. If you sat "hunkered down" between two couches with a mattress over your head for thirty hours, with the wind howling and rainwater dripping down your inside walls, it might be difficult for you to have positive feelings. But that's okay, because it's not the attitude or feelings that are important. **It is whether you THINK positive THOUGHTS!**

Thinking positive thoughts even when you feel less than positive will create automatic changes in the way you respond in your brain at the non-conscious level. You can't create a positive attitude out of nowhere. You change your attitude by changing something other than your feelings. It is the thoughts that count! If you change your thoughts, you will change your brain, which will change your life.

It is impossible to always have a PMA. Thank goodness, now we know scientifically that you don't always have to have one. For a while, you are going to be on a day-to-day basis—more of a professional observer of how you think and what you think and you do need to generate positive thoughts.

There are ways to generate the flow of positive thought neuron patterns in your brain even under the worst conditions.

How do you think positive thoughts? You act. If you talk to an Academy Award winning actor about how they can generate those real tears in a movie, they will tell you that they think about situations that would make them cry. Those situations aren't really occurring at the conscious level. But the non-conscious level doesn't know they aren't real. 5/6 of the brain takes those thoughts as real and generates that new feeling with the tears flowing.

> **A positive attitude is not always necessary, but positive thoughts are!**

If you just act out positive thoughts, even if you're not feeling them, you can reach greater levels of achievement. One of the greatest brain research discoveries of all time is that 5/6 of your brain's thinking is done at the non-conscious level. The thinking that occurs at the non-conscious level is taken as real whether or not you feel that way at the conscious level. That's why a sad movie seems really sad to you and a scary movie seems scary, even though you know it's not real. So if you can generate positive thoughts, whether they are imagined or real doesn't matter. To 5/6 of your brain, they will be taken as real. Change your thoughts toward the positive, change your brain, and change your life.

Brain Apples Implant #6: The one thing that you absolutely must do before you undertake any new task or you are doomed to fail.

If you want quality performance, whether it is a great sales presentation or a better athletic skill, you must first visualize the perfect performance of that action before you physically undertake that behavior.

Researchers have discovered that the more you send an impulse down a given neuron pattern, the more likely and easier it is to go down that same pattern again, and the lower the firing threshold is for that thought pattern, so that it's more likely to take that same path again and again.

The first time you take a new or overgrown pathway in a rain forest, it's pretty hard! Even with a sharp machete. But the next time is easier, and so is the next time. And the next time is still easier. **Well, what if, when you start a new task, you don't visualize it but just go ahead and physically attempt it?** Your first effort is not going to be anywhere near perfect, is it? Yet you have just created a pathway that is more likely for your future neuron firings to go down, but it's not the path you want.

So, in order for you to perfect a new physical skill and find that path, you must first:

- Visualize the perfect movements of that skill in your brain, creating neuron pathways that become easier to follow; then visualize perfect performance of that practice or act within your brain.

I'm reminded of the story, recounted by Zig Ziglar, Jack Canfield and others, of a man who was a prisoner of war in Vietnam for seven years ...

Before he went to Vietnam, he was a tremendously skilled golfer. When he was released, he came back to the United States and a reporter asked him, "How did you survive in prison camps for seven years?" The soldier said, "I played golf." The reporter, puzzled, said, "What do you mean you played golf?"

"I played golf every single day. Every day I imagined that I got up and went to a golf course—the most famous, wonderful golf courses in the world—and I shot a round of golf each and every day. I went through every shot. I went through tying my shoes. I went through walking to the first hole, feeling the dew on the grass as I placed my ball on the tee. I even imagined throwing up blades of grass to see which way the wind was blowing. I imagined every shot every day for seven years." The day after the soldier came home, he played golf. Now, you and I know what happens to our golf game if we don't play very much. It goes down the pooper doesn't it? Mine does. Yet on that first round of golf, after having visualized playing golf in his mind for seven years, the man shot a 73, one stroke over par (which the professionals consider to be near perfect).

You must visualize, visualize, visualize before you undertake a new activity. Before you turn it over to the automated functioning in your non-conscious brain, you must create neuron pathways that are as nearly perfect as possible so that the firings in your brain when you're making the actual physical movements will be more likely to go down the nearly perfect pathway.

*To demonstrate this, there have been several studies of people shooting foul shots in basketball, because it's so easy to measure the effects of visualization in this activity. In one study, there were 4 groups. For 21 days, one group only practiced physically shooting foul shots. A second group never touched a basketball but, for 21 days they visualized shooting foul shots. A third group both visualized and physically practiced and the fourth group did nothing for 21 days. I'm sure you can guess the results. The group that did nothing did very poorly. The group that physically practiced did pretty well. The group that only visualized, and never touched a basketball, did within 6/10 of 1% as well as the group that practiced with a basketball. The group that both visualized and physically practiced did over **27% better** than any of the other groups. Whether getting ready for a physical feat or any other performance, your results will soar if you first visualize your act at least 7-14 days.*

> **Visualize before you undertake a new activity.**

So that old cliché, "practice makes perfect," is not really reliable, is it? An even worse cliché, "perfect practice makes perfect" is not correct either. What is most correct is "visualize perfect practice," then go perform deliberate and perfect practice, then perform your project or goal. Visualization is absolutely necessary before you undertake any new activity or your activity, skill and goal will be doomed to fail.

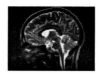

Brain Apples Implant #7: To your health!

How many times have you heard the toast, at a wedding, party or celebration, just before taking a drink, "To your health"? In the *Brain Apples Blueprint* program, "to your health" means something entirely different.

A study, done at the University of Pittsburgh Hospital for 30 months, studied all the patients recovering from surgical procedures. *The University hospital is built in a quadrangular shape. Some of the rooms face north, some face south, some east, and some west. What they discovered over that 30-month period was that post-operative patients in the rooms facing south needed, on average, 22% less pain medication during their recovery period than patients in rooms facing any one of the other directions.*

What could these findings be attributed to? Of course, rooms facing south in the northern part of our country would receive more sunlight when the sun hangs lower in the sky during the winter. And so it could be very easy to draw the conclusion that sunlight reduces pain. Well, that's not the right conclusion. The correct conclusion is that, because those rooms facing south had more natural daylight, they were brighter than those rooms that faced north, east or west. As a result of those rooms being brighter, the patients had more positive thoughts and feelings and needed less pain medication. What does this mean for you and me? It means that brighter lighting or more natural light on your walls and in your homes and offices contribute to your overall good health.

Is this concept limited to health? Not by a long shot. Another study found that students who were taking standardized tests did better, on average, in more well-lit classrooms than those students in rooms that were not as well lit.

Change your thinking, change your brain, and change your life, and you can influence your health!

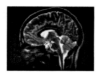

Brain Apples Implant #8: Be a Big Baby!

Have you ever watched a child learn to walk? I have five grandsons, and they, like most children, learned to walk in two ways:

- First, by watching us and then trying to repeat that action.

- Second and more importantly, I think, by falling (failing).

Falling/failing involves *doing* and not just *watching*, so you learn a skill better when you attempt to do it, even if you don't achieve it.

Children learn new tasks by falling down again and again. The more they fall, the quicker and better they learn how to stand up and walk. Each time a young child falls, new neuron connections are formed in their brain. As those neuron connections are being formed, their brain learns the appropriate pattern of neurons to fire in order to walk. To succeed, sometimes adults also must first fail.

> **"Nothing good works well the first time!"**
>
> *-Brian Tracy*

It's important to notice carefully that I didn't say, *'You're a failure.'* You can never be a failure. But can you fall/fail? Absolutely! And the sooner you fall down, the better. By falling, you'll learn the correct neuron pathways quicker, and generate new DSP connections and neuron pathways that will lead you to greater success.

One way to do this is by **visualizing**, and the second way is by **failing**. So when you do fall, get excited, fail fast, fall fast, and fall many times, because that's how you'll learn to succeed and that's how you form the neuron connections that will lead to success.

> **The faster you fail, the quicker you reach success.**

Many people are afraid of failing because they take it personally. They think it makes them a failure. That's impossible. The Creator generated no failures. But you certainly can and must fail. There is no need, scientifically, to fear failing because failing is good. Failing is positive and allows your brain to generate new neuron pattern connections to learn what's required for success. It's one of the most masterful ways that new DSP connections are formed in the brain. But if you fail at a new task, you will only succeed if **after that failing, you analyze it.** Allow your non-conscious brain to bring you information about that action or event so your conscious brain can learn from it.

When you fall down, it will lead to new connections that will lead you closer to the perfection you seek in a new skill. **Don't forget that you will never reach perfection -- it's impossible. What you want to reach is success. And success requires failing.**

Brain Apples Implant #9: Newton's Law and the Final Four.

We all procrastinate, and most of us hate it. We agonize over it, and feel guilty doing it. I am going to set you free with this implant!

Procrastination does not really exist as most of us define it. Procrastination is not failing. It doesn't make you a failure. Procrastination really is just a choice. You make a choice for one action instead of another. You set priorities with your actions, and you chose a different priority than the one you feel you should have chosen. We do this every single day. We are always making choices of one activity over another.

Motivational experts tell us if we want to overcome procrastination, we have to make a list of everything we have to do, and then we have to tackle the toughest task first. Hog manure! That won't work. It flies in the face of the laws of physics. We're talking about science-based techniques to advance your achievement skills, so **let's find a way to eliminate and, once and for all, overcome procrastination.**

When the game had ended and his team had lost, I heard a very positive coach say, "Well, we didn't really lose that game. We just happened to have been behind when time ran out." In today's culture there are always going to be more to get done in a day than the day has time.

I have a solution. Sir Isaac Newton had many laws of physics. One of his laws was that a body at rest tends to stay at rest; a body in motion tends to stay in motion.

I am going to give you a somewhat different, yet very successful approach to overcoming procrastination so that it is never a problem for you again.

If you are faced with several tasks, list those tasks on a sheet of paper. Do not prioritize them. Draw brackets connecting the two at the top, Go down through the list until you have completed brackets connecting the next two, and the next two, etc.

Then go back to the top of your list and look at those first two tasks. Whichever one of those tasks is the **easiest**, whichever would require the least amount of energy and the least amount of effort, move that task out to the right to the next bracket as if it were the winner of that match or that game. Go through your entire list of tasks and do the same thing with each one—moving the easiest task out to the winner's row to the right.

After you have completed the first round, do the same thing with the winning tasks. Take the top two and draw brackets around them. Then choose the **easiest** of those and move it out as the winner. When you get down to the final four and the final game, the semifinals, and the finals, you only have two tasks left. Choose the **easiest** and then do that task.

Before you start this, you must commit that, whatever the easiest task is, you are going to do it. But that is very easy to do. We are not going to do the toughest task; we'll start with the easiest task. Why, because of Newton's Law.

Which do you suppose is easier to get into motion—a train with 120 cars filled with coal or a train with one passenger car? Choose the task that is going to require the least amount of energy to get you moving.

Why not go for your toughest task after you have already built momentum and speed on the easier tasks? Isaac Newton had it right. **Get your body in motion and it will stay in motion.**

Sometimes I will do something small that isn't even related to anything on my list just to get the momentum started! Take out the trash, or wipe the fingerprints off the door, anything that requires motion and gets me up and moving! The easiest task on my list will then keep me moving. Then go to your next easiest task and do that. Then you go to another one and another one. Soon your momentum is flying forward fast. You've overcome procrastination, but not by tackling the most complicated high-energy task first. This idea is based on the law of physics -- **apply Newton's Law and procrastination will be a thing of the past for you.**

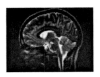

Brain Apples Implant #10: *Here comes the devil— let him in! Discomfort is required!*

The devil is that nasty part of your brain called the Amygdala. It's a little almond-shaped part of the brain that sits at the end of the Hippocampus. You have two amygdalae, one on each side of the brain. Your amygdala has an extremely important function—**it's the part of the brain that recognizes fear, danger, stress, anxiety and emotions and instantly, without thinking, responds.**

The role of the amygdala is to recognize those emotional impulses and send signals to other parts of your brain and body to release hormones and neurotransmitters to control the fear and overcome danger. The amygdala is a very powerful and good thing to have functioning properly. If you're suddenly faced with a high level of danger, your amygdala recognizes that danger, orders the release of epinephrine, or adrenaline, which increases exponentially the strength in your muscles to allow you to either fight or flee (the fight or flight response). That's all done by order of the amygdala. Releasing hormones when you become fearful or stressful or filled with anxiety happens automatically!

However, in the achievement sense, the amygdala is not your friend—it's the devil. The major role of the amygdala is to keep you at the easiest, safest, status quo level because it senses you are safest there.

34

Negativity bias

But when you're trying to accomplish new things, trying to step out of your comfort zone to attempt new skills, and you want to perfect those new skills to advance your achievement levels, the amygdala is no longer your friend, it's the devil. When you're attempting a new task or perfecting a new skill, you're stressful and uncomfortable. The amygdala senses that and immediately sends soldiers out to your brain and body saying, "BAM, let's grab our person and bring him back into his comfort zone."

But if you, over time, repeat and repeat efforts toward those new skills, you become desensitized with each repeated effort. The skill becomes more of a habit and your amygdala no longer recognizes it as something that requires pulling you back and keeping you at status quo.

How long does it take? 21-30 days. You've heard that many times, haven't you? It will probably take you a good 3-4 weeks of effort on a new task before you feel comfortable enough that stress and anxiety are not created trying to keep you in your comfort zone. If you recognize this as being a totally physiological event, rather than a psychological, "I can't accomplish that" type of act, you will use habituation and sensitization (the tendency of a response to decrease or increase with repeated exposure to a stimulus) to your advantage. If you learn to apply H&S, you'll understand that when you're trying something new, your amygdala is going to try to stop you. It's the devil, but let the devil in so that, down the road as you desensitize yourself through practice, the amygdala will no longer act. If you try it today, and then don't try it again for another 21 days, you're not training or desensitizing your amygdala and you're not going to have the kind of success you're after.

I've been a professional speaker for 35-40 years. I started speaking back in high school, and it carried through to my career as an attorney and a judge. After retiring from my law career 18 years ago, I have been speaking professionally all over this country to small groups and groups as large as 9,000 people. I love it, but I've got to be honest with you. When I'm going to give a speech to a new group or use a new speech, I get very uncomfortable. Why? Because my amygdala is trying to save me, protect me. It sees that I'm out of my comfort zone. It sees that I'm stressed and filled with anxiety. It will release the neurotransmitters and hormones to bring me back to the status quo.

When I feel uncomfortable with any new task, that's the time to get excited and embrace the discomfort. When you do, and as you practice, the discomfort levels recognized by your amygdala will be reduced, and it will no longer try to keep you from changing. That's fantastic news, isn't it?

******

I was recently contacted by a well-known author who wanted to include a quote from me in his book about success and achievement. He wanted to know what I thought were the secrets of successful people. One of the success secrets I gave him is that successful people are constantly doing things they're not sure they know how to do. I get so excited now when I am out of my comfort zone because it means I'm learning or trying something new. It means I'm desensitizing that stinker, the amygdala, so it will allow me to step outside of, or expand my comfort zone.

- Get out of your comfort zone.

- Stand backward in an elevator.

- Shake the hand of everybody on a bus.

- Wear one brown shoe and one black shoe when you're giving a speech.

Step out of your comfort zone on a regular basis and you will desensitize and habituate your amygdala to leave you alone when you're going after a new task.

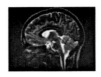

Brain Apples Implant #11: If discomfort is not recognized, it becomes FEAR!

If you don't see discomfort as simply a step outside your comfort zone that you can celebrate, the discomfort can develop rapidly, expand exponentially, and spread like a virus into that awful 4-letter word: **F-E-A-R.**

What happens if you don't recognize that your amygdala is lying to you? As I said earlier, it creates discomfort, stress and anxiety and tries to pull you back into your comfort zone to keep you from changing, or from possibly getting hurt. The amygdala is in the reptilian portion of the brain, which is the non-cortex, non-deductive, non-logical thinking portion. It knows no better. It senses the stress and, it explodes to try to keep you safe.

If you allow discomfort to spread unrecognized into fear, then you have a problem. I'm not talking about little smidgens of discomfort like the butterflies I get before I make a speech. I'm talking about large amounts of great fear. You have to consciously recognize that discomfort is not fear; it is simply discomfort from being out of your comfort zone. Don't forget that neurons are biochemical, electrical impulses. They are real. Your stress can become physical and you can be in deep trouble as well if you allow discomfort to turn into fear.

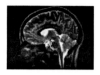

Brain Apples Implant #12: High levels of fear block action.

If discomfort grows into fear and that fear is allowed to rapidly grow, it will take your anxiety meter up into the red zone and your motor will blow up. When there are high levels of fear, the flow of neuron impulses, and the creation of new DSP connections stops. The fear will freeze you in your tracks, making you incapable of performing. You have to recognize that discomfort is a great thing, if it's recognized as simply a step out of your comfort zone and not misdiagnosed as fear that can keep you from taking action.

Your amygdala releases discomfort and causes fear. The discomfort can block the impulses in your brain that send signals to your muscles to perform in a certain way, and to your brain (i.e., your cortex) to think in a certain way -- to keep you from acting, speaking or moving in a certain way. High levels of fear can grow into red-zone anxiety impulses that will, in fact, block the flow of impulses you are firing to complete your action or achievement. When discomfort grows to unchecked fear, it reaches a threshold that sets off an alarm in your amygdala for it to instantly order all parts of your brain and body to STOP ALL ACTIONS!

But the fear is simple to overcome. Just recognize that your discomfort is a fantastic thing. It means you're growing, it means you're achieving. Force yourself, upon recognition to **THINK of discomfort not fear.**

Acknowledge discomfort! Embrace discomfort! Let it in and use it in a 21-30 day process to tame your amygdala. Once you understand (in your cortex) how the amygdala releases these hormones and neurotransmitters to fake you out and make you feel uncomfortable, you'll be able to embrace that discomfort as a good thing.

> *FEAR places no limits on your achievements.*

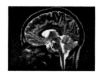

Brain Apples Implant #13: *Learn to trust the darkness.*

Every time we have an experience, learn something new, or stimulate our brain, neuron patterns are created and a memory of that experience is stored somewhere in our brain—perfectly. But, we just do not always have access at the CONSCIOUS level to all those memories.

When you get an idea or a solution to a problem comes up to your conscious level from your non-conscious brain those—seemingly "out-of-the-blue" intuitive hunch-like impulses—are coming to you based on information available only at the non-conscious level. Therefore, those answers, or ideas will not be tainted by your conscious thoughts, which are based solely on your perception of what is real, not necessarily what is actually real. When you take action based on a thought or idea that comes to you through your non-conscious brain, it is a much more reliable solution.

Therefore, learn to **"trust the darkness" of your non-conscious brain!** If every memory you have is stored perfectly in the memory storage areas in your brain, it would be in your best interest to learn and experience all you can because the more memories that are available when your non-conscious is searching for an answer, the more likely that answer will be terrifically good for you.

So never stop learning, and always trust your intuition. It's based on the perfect information and perfect memories, even if you can't always recall it at the conscious level.

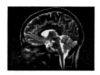

Brain Apples Implant #14: Bad habits can't be broken.

If you have a habit that is holding you back or keeping you from achieving as much as you would like to achieve, you can't break it. Once those neuron patterns have connected, it is nearly impossible to break them. It would take years for those connections to atrophy from lack of use, so you can never break that bad habit. It is impossible, physiologically.

Oh well, I take that all back. I guess you *could* physically break a bad habit. It would require brain surgery to do it, though. You see, the wiring in the brain is color coded, so you could hire a surgeon to cut open your brain and clip all the yellow wires. BOOM! You would be rid of that bad habit, but that's the only way. Pretty silly, huh?

What is a bad habit?

... A series of neuron patterns from your brain's non-conscious storage areas that will continually fire because you have fired them so many times in the past.

The more a thought or action goes down the neuron pathway, the easier it is for the thought or action to go that way again. When it has gone that way enough times, it becomes automated and automatic. It's a physical, physiological and biological reaction.

So what *can* you do to overcome bad habits? You have to change the flow of the river, the neuron pathways that those impulses go down. You can't stop those neurons from firing. Instead, you need to create a new riverbed when they start to fire.

Create a new thought, a new direction for those neuron impulses to flow down, and then repeat that new direction, intentionally, even if it is a lie, even if you have to force yourself to do so. Not just once or twice, but for at least 21 days.

> *Thoughts are real things—biochemical electrical impulses. Therefore you cannot break a bad habit.*

It *does* take effort to change your life. If you're looking for a quick fix, it's not going to happen. You can't change without changing your thoughts. If you want to eliminate a bad habit, you can't destroy it or break it; you have to make new neuron pathways.

You can have some habits that you *want* to change, of course, such as smoking, that I'm not able to help you with. However, once that physical addiction has been overcome with knowledge and effort on your part, you can change the habits that used to be associated with smoking into new habits— with about 30 days of sweat and tears. But it can be done. Weight control, quit smoking, achieving any great thing!

> *You don't break your habits, you change your habits.*

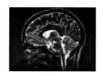

Brain Apples Implant #15: **_Your prefrontal cortex is your achieving friend_**.

When you make a mistake, a PET scan will show that your prefrontal cortex, in the front part of your frontal lobe, is firing neuron patterns based on that mistake. There are sections of your prefrontal cortex that fire only if you have made a mistake. **The prefrontal cortex neurons are searching for information to help you to fix that error.** The neurons fire that way automatically, but you need to do something after you have made that mistake to help your prefrontal cortex.

The firings that occur when you make a mistake concentrate on creating neuron patterns of images or pictures that you _do not_ want. Remember that we said that what you think about at the non-conscious level, the pictures you generate there, are taken as real by your non-conscious brain. If you concentrate on what you do _not_ want after you make a mistake, your prefrontal cortex will believe or form neuron connections indicating that that is what you _do_ want, and it will be much more complicated and difficult to overcome that mistake.

For example, if you are a golfer and you miss a 3-foot putt for a $100 bet, don't ask your brain to ensure that you don't miss that putt again. Concentrate on what you _do_ want: making a good tempo and rhythm stroke, getting a straight follow-through, keeping your eye on the ball. Don't even turn and look at the hole. Don't concentrate on what you do not want because your prefrontal cortex will assume it should fix your mistake by giving you the pictures you are generating. This phenomenon is similar to the "don't spill the milk" example. When you tell your child, "Whatever you do, don't spill the milk," their non-conscious brain sees a picture of spilling the milk as if that was what you wanted.

After you make a mistake, study your mistake and then concentrate on what you *do* want, not on what you do *not* want. ("Son, I want you to enjoy all your milk, so hold the glass with two hands until you see the bottom of the glass!")

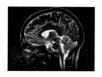

Brain Apples Implant #16: Visualize the good stuff.

When you form a mental image of something in your brain, the visual area of your occipital lobe—the part of your brain that interprets sight—is more active. (Doctors can see this with brain-scanning equipment.) It is as active as if you had seen the actual object. Therefore, it is vitally important that you exercise and develop your visualization skills. You have to positively see your goals, ambitions and achievements on a regular basis to help your brain out. Your brain will think it is seeing your goals in reality, in real time, if you visualize your goals. And, after a mistake, visualize what you *want*, not what you do *not* want. **Visualize. Visualize. Visualize.**

Involve all your senses in that visualization—sight, touch, smell, taste, and hearing. If one of your goals is to buy a new car, go see that car, sit in it, touch it, smell it, listen to the engine so that when you later visualize the car, your brain will involve all your senses, and more powerful, more focused and stronger neuron connections are created. The more you involve your senses, the more connections are formed, and you are going to get automatic firing neurons related to that goal from then on.

Don't just create mental images of your goals. Live them. See them. Smell them. Touch them. Hear them. Every day, create those mental images as if your goals were reality. Play out scenes in your mind as if your goals have already been achieved, including their looks, smells, touch, taste, and sounds. The more of your senses you involve, the more directly your non-conscious brain will go to work to get you exactly that.

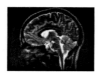

Brain Apples Implant #17: Change your brain -- change your life.

There are several science-based books that I think are must-reads for you to generate the kind of achievement skills you want to have for the rest of your life. One of those books is *Change Your Brain, Change Your Life*, by Dr. Daniel Amen. It is a tremendous book. You must read it. You can use that book along with our *Brain Apples Blueprint* program to take your achievements to their highest levels. It's a short and powerful read. Some of the quotes and information in Dr. Amen's book will just blow you away in their helpfulness to have science-based, advanced achievement skills.

As you read Amen's book, highlight the important parts and then write out by hand your notes from those highlighted parts the second time you go through the book. If you read a book that way, you are creating new neuron connections in your brain that give you a picture of just how important the information is. You are visualizing what the words express on the pages as if they were real at that instant. So get his book and then make it come alive!

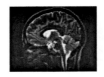

Brain Apples Implant #18: Willpower is vastly overrated.

Willpower is Overrated: The Real Brain Science Secret to Persistence and Overcoming Procrastination is the title of a report I wrote that has been published in various journals, and is available on the Internet. If you haven't had a chance to read it, email me and I'll send you the link so you can read it as a part of this implant lesson.

Your willpower is seated in your conscious thoughts. Your desires, self-discipline and willpower all reside in conscious neuron patterns. Remember that your conscious neurons and thoughts only make up 1/6 of your brain's thinking. Your willpower originates in this 1/6 section. 5/6 of your brain is thinking at the non-conscious level 24 hours a day, 7 days a week. Trust your non-conscious to work for you. It never takes a day off!

Let me reiterate: Your conscious efforts, your desire for success and your willpower, generate from only 1/6 of your brain's power. You must learn that, even if you have tremendous willpower, you may not reach your goals; you may keep hitting the wall or you may keep bouncing off it even though your willpower is 10 times greater than the willpower of others who may have reached their goals.

What's the difference? The real power lies in your non-conscious thoughts—5/6 of your brain's power and thinking! 83% of your actions are directed NOT by your willpower, but by your non-conscious thoughts!

Do you want to know how to increase your productivity 500%? Do the math. If you are attempting to reach your goals only by using willpower, you will be woefully short of your goal. If you are firing on only 1/6 of your motor cylinders, you are going to come in last. If you want to multiply that effort by 5 times, you must involve your non-conscious thinking. Unfortunately, at the conscious level, you are not even aware of what your non-conscious thoughts are, yet they control your power and your actions. What you have to do is get your conscious goals, willpower and desire in sync with your non-conscious goals.

Willpower is still important to help "flip the switch" to getting started on some action. But your power to complete any task that your willpower helps you start resides in 5/6 of your brain called your non-conscious brain.

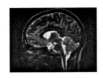

Brain Apples Implant #19: *Muster your entire army.*

When you think about a task or a goal, and it dominates your conscious thinking, automatic neuron patterns begin firing in the non-conscious portion of your brain, seeking neuron patterns from your memory banks to bring the plans, ideas or solutions for your dominant thoughts at the conscious level.

In other words, whatever your dominant thoughts are, your non-conscious brain goes to work to bring you a solution or conclusion or level of achievement to reach that dominant thought. The more you fill your thoughts with what it is you *want* to achieve—not what you do *not* want to achieve—the more you are going to muster the armies of your non-conscious brain to bring you the proper actions and solutions.

If you dwell at the conscious level on "worry," what can go wrong, or what you don't want, your non-conscious brain will not go to work for you to seek out what you do want. Remember, your non-conscious can't tell real from imagined; everything is taken literally. Muster your full army by filling your conscious thoughts with exactly, precisely, specifically, the results you do want.

If you want a new home, don't just have thoughts in your conscious brain about that new home; picture yourself standing in front of it. See the house in minute detail in your images and thoughts, from the type of roof, the color of the shingles or the texture of the tile. How many windows are on the front of the house? Do they have separate panes of glass or are they all one piece? Do you have shutters? Do you have woodwork around the windows? Completely describe what you want so you can muster your full army of neuron patterns at your non-conscious level where your most powerful arsenal resides.

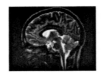

Brain Apples Implant #20: The brain can't store energy.

This Brain Apples Implant is one of the lessons at the very heart of your ability to reach high levels of advanced achievements over the rest of your life. You need to understand this Implant and use it in many, many areas of your life.

As I said earlier, if you use willpower to get you started on a task, and if you muster your full army by filling your conscious thoughts with what you want, your non-conscious brain will go to work to find you solutions and methods to reach that goal.

But here is the problem: **When your non-conscious brain comes up with a solution to the problem or challenge before you, when that thought or solution arrives at your conscious level, it's placed in your short-term memory,** and it may arrive not on your schedule and not when you're looking for it. So you may not recognize it! And if that's not bad enough, the answer or idea is placed in short-term memory that will only fire for a very short time before its shut down (usually less than 45 seconds!) and you "forget" the idea.

It is vitally important for you to understand that memory is an active process, not passive. What that means is that you must take some action to move that neuron pattern from short-term memory and place it into long-term memory, BEFORE it stops firing! It will not go there automatically.

> **You must take ACTION to put your ideas into long-term memory!**

Certain situations send ideas and thoughts to long-term memory instantly, but they are not of our creation. They are placed there by the Creator, or they are there as a result of a trauma or tragedy. Events related to extremely emotional circumstances do go directly to long-term memory.

However, if you want all other ideas, thoughts and neuron patterns to go to long-term memory, you must take some action to place them there because the brain can't store energy.

The most important thing to understand about this is that your brain knows it can't store energy. So, as it matures, it starts conserving energy for those mandatory needs or emergencies.

One means by which your brain conserves energy is sending neuron impulses to short-term memory. They will continue to fire there in short-term memory for 7 seconds to 12 minutes. Then, they will stop firing to conserve energy. The average time that a firing impulse is stored in short-term memory, before it will stop firing, is 37-47 seconds. If an idea comes to you from your non-conscious brain, unless you take some active process or procedure to put that memory into some form of long-term storage, those neuron patterns, that idea, that solution will be gone forever!

Have you ever awakened in the middle of the night with a great idea? Say you have had a problem at work and haven't figured out a solution. Then, BAM! You wake up in the middle of the night with an idea that solves that problem. What happens to that idea if you don't write it down or take some action to put it into long-term memory? The idea stops firing and those neurons are gone forever; when you wake up in the morning, you won't be able to recall what you were thinking about.

What can you do to counteract this problem or this challenge? **Take action to put the ideas into long-term memory!** You can do one or two things. You can store it in artificial memory by writing it down or putting it on a recorder. Or you could use repetition or association with other things that are already in long-term memory so there is a connection. The more emotion involved with that repetition or association, the stronger those neuron connections will be in your long-term memory and the more likely you will be able to recall that information.

I always have a digital voice recorder at my side. I won't be without it anywhere. If I'm sleeping, it is on the nightstand. If I'm in the bathroom, it goes to the bathroom with me! I want to have the means to put any idea that comes to me from my non-conscious brain into long-term memory, whether it is artificial memory or my brain's true memory. I want to be able to store it.

If you are taking our bonus course on how to generate money-making ideas and put them on the Internet to make money, you know that is one of the very important principles: You train your brain to recognize when money-making ideas come up from your non-conscious level. They are worthless if you don't put them into long-term memory before they stop firing.

Memory is an active process, not an automatic one. It requires your efforts because the brain can't store energy.

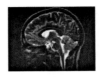

Brain Apples Implant #21: Memory is an active process-the details.

As we've said, you must take action to store a memory or thought in your brain's long-term storage center. There are three actions you can take to store a long-term memory:

1) **Repetition**. Repetition forms new DSPs in the brain. As the number of new DSPs increases, your brain will increase the importance of the thought you are repeating and make you more likely to recall it in the future. This is how you're able to remember a new acquaintance's name.

Why is it important that you remember the names of the people you meet? That should go without saying if you are in business or have customers or want to seek greater achievements.

When you meet someone for the first time, you could say, "Hi. I'm Doug Bench, and your name is? Oh, Jim. Nice to meet you, Jim. Jim, hold on one second."

Jim, Jim, Jim, Jim, Jim, Jim, Jim, Jim. Unfortunately, you can't just repeat a person's name ad nauseam. You aren't going to be talking to that person very long if that's the means you use to remember their name.

But you can repeat their name back to them in the

course of your conversation. For example, "What kind of work do you do, Jim? Do you have children Jim?" Do that enough and the name is placed in long-term memory.

2) **By association.** Association means connecting a name with something you have already stored in long-term memory. For example, the other day, as I was teaching a seminar, I was giving an example of association by introducing myself to a gentleman. "Hi. I'm Doug Bench." He said his name was Noel. Interestingly enough, Noel had white hair, a white mustache and a white goatee. Snow white hair, snow white mustache and beard, snow, white, Christmas, Noel. Bingo! Things associated with a white Christmas and snow and the word Noel, which is associated with Christmas—all those other things were already stored in my long-term memory. So when I see his white hair from now on, it will trigger these associative neuron connections to fire. White hair, snow white, snow, Christmas, white Christmas. His name is Noel.

3) We really can't control the third way things get placed in long-term memory: **through traumatic, tragic or emotional experience.** The experience doesn't always have to be negative, however. Some very positive experiences can be traumatic, such as watching the birth of your first child.

If trauma or emotions, at a very high level, are involved in an experience, the Creator has made our brain in such a way that those memories will bypass short-term memory and go directly to long-term memory. Those people who are old enough will remember exactly where we were when we found out that President John F. Kennedy had been assassinated. I can tell you where I was standing, who I was standing with, what time of day it was, the shirt I had on, the books I had under my arm, and even what I had had for lunch that day, because that news was a very emotional experience. As I watched the news, the neuron patterns went directly into my long-term memory. The birth of your children is often like that. You can consciously help move events into long-term memory with this method because the connections being formed when you are emotional are stronger, there are more of them, and they are longer lasting.

Humor also can create emotions, inject some into your conversation and it will help you to memorize! **Memory requires action; it is not passive.** Stop beating yourself up for forgetting names, for forgetting where you put your glasses, for forgetting to return a call, because all of those events first fire in short-term memory. If you don't take some action to move that information from short-term into long-term memory by your actions, those neurons will stop firing anywhere from 7 seconds to 12 minutes (average time is less than a minute). You have to take action to retain those memories and stop being negative about yourself. Now you have the tools to make yourself good with names. But you only have 45 seconds!

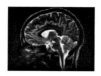

Brain Apples Implant #22: Combine brain science secrets with your sakes pitch and double your sales!

Are you in sales? Do you give presentations or estimates to customers who get 2-3 other estimates and then make a decision on who gets the job? If you learn and apply these brain-research based secrets in YOUR presentation, you will more than double your chances of getting the sale, even if you're the highest bidder!

First, you must put your customer's name into long-term memory! When you are making a presentation to a customer, you must be able to repeat their name while looking them in the eyes, without having to refer to a note in front of you. If your customer sees you doing that, they are going to think, with emotion, that they are not important enough for you to recall their name, and you have lost the sale already! People buy based on emotion, not facts! You MUST, therefore, **appeal to their emotion.**

Whenever you look into someone's eyes during the conversation, repeat their name. Brain Research tells us that when this happens, endorphins are released across each synapse firing in that person's brain at that moment. This is automatic! They are not consciously aware of this, but it always happens!

What are endorphins?

Endorphins are chemical compounds produced by the pituitary gland and hypothalamus that, when released, have a pain-inhibiting, analgesic effect on the brain that creates a feeling of pleasure, comfort or well-being. Do you see the power in this? And, if you are using their name during your presentation, particularly during an emotion-triggering subject (such as the safety features of your swimming pool design to keep their young children safe), the new DSP connections being formed in their brain are stronger, longer-lasting, and more easily recalled and fired again.

Therefore, whenever you repeat someone's name, they have feelings of comfort, well-being, and pleasure created by their brain, which can be translated into trust for you. Whenever someone feels comfortable, they are more likely to trust you and/or more likely to feel they have known you for a long time. Both of which help make it more likely that you will get the sale!

Now here comes the best part: Let's say that you are a pool contractor and your potential customer is getting three bids for the pool they want to build. You present your estimate, sales pitch, benefits and features before the other contractors (although it really doesn't matter what order it's done in.) During your presentation, since you have read and applied the secret brain-research-based strategies from this book, you have put their name into long-term memory and used it 8-12 times while looking them in the eye, especially during the emotion-triggering topics. All during your presentation, they are having feelings of comfort and pleasure because you have triggered those feelings in their brain!

The next day, the customer get estimates from contractors B and C, which are both lower than your bid, and the customer tells you that they are going to think it over and let you know. On Saturday, when they sit down at the kitchen table to think about each of your presentations and bids, 5/6 of their brain (the non-conscious brain) will be firing EXACTLY the same neuron patterns that were fired when you were actually in the room with them! In fact, their non-conscious brain will think you are there! Their non-conscious brain takes everything as happening in real time, and can't distinguish real from imagined.

The same endorphins that were released in their brain when you were there will be released again when they think about you, even though you are long gone fishin'. Therefore, when they review your presentation later, they will again feel pleasure, comfort and trust! Your chances of getting the sale just skyrocketed, even though you were the highest bidder and not even there now.

The customer will think, "I can trust him"; "I feel like I know him;" "I don't know why I want him to do the work; it's just a feeling I have!" That feeling is what you created in their brain. Trust neuroscience for your greatest sales presentations!

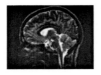

Brain Apples Implant #23: Form a mastermind group.

The idea of mastermind groups has been around since Napoleon Hill's book, *Think and Grow Rich*, written in 1939. Today, **why a mastermind group is so important is backed by neuroscience research.**

A mastermind group is a group of 3-6 like-thinking people, including yourself, that you get together with, even if it's just once a month, to brainstorm and bounce ideas off, ask for critical support or constructive criticism, or go over your goals. They will give you support for your goals, you will support theirs. It's tremendously empowering to be in a mastermind group.

You know the expression "can't see the forest for the trees"? Sometimes you try so hard in your conscious forest of neurons to find a solution to a problem that the real solution coming up from the non-conscious brain can't get through "all the trees." If you have the perspective of someone else whose conscious neurons are not being clogged up, a support group might see through the trees for you.

The American psychologist, Abraham Maslow, developed a pyramid of human needs that most of us have seen. At the top of that pyramid is self-actualization., Maslow said, **"Self-actualization is a feeling of accomplishment."** This feeling of self-actualization and accomplishment can be generated for you from the input of people outside your brain who are in similar situations and who are supportive of you.

Let's look at the science of accomplishment to see why it is so important that you get that feeling of "Wow, I did it!" It can come from the other people in your mastermind group whose opinions you respect and trust. What happens physiologically is this: When someone praises you, it causes the release of certain neurotransmitters in your brain that cause the release of endorphins.

Endorphins inhibit the flow of pain impulses and increase the flow of pleasure impulses. Physiologically, you will feel pleasure when members of your mastermind group praise you. That is vitally important to your self-confidence and your willingness to try things outside your comfort zone. Not to mention the fact that, together with others in your group, you can come up with money-making ideas for all of you.

One of the reasons people feel so good after they go to a self-development seminar is that there are like-minded people at that seminar who help fulfill each other's feelings or needs for self-actualization. With that release of endorphins, you feel good.

Get yourself a mastermind group --

> ➢ Find 3-6 people who think like you do, who are positive like you are, who will be supportive of your ideas, and who will supply constructive (not destructive) criticism. They will not ever attempt

65

to keep you from achieving your goals. They will simply be constructive in their support of your efforts and maybe make some suggestions of things to try that you have not tried. That can be very beneficial from a scientific point of view and from a self-actualization, psychological point of view.

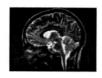

Brain Apples Implant #24: Always step up in your mastermind group, never down!

Even more important than forming a mastermind group is forming that group made up of people who are in the position you want to get to, people who have achieved at or above your level. That will greatly help you grow!

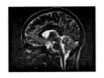

Brain Apples Implant #25: Feelings are physical reactions to your thoughts.

(This implant deserves at least three stars.) If you get a reaction to something —a cry, a blush, a flushed feeling, a flushed face, red-faced embarrassment, pain in the side, anger—it's probably a physiological reaction to a thought you are having, or have had, at the conscious level.

Feelings of being unhappy or angry are based on your thoughts and are, therefore, totally controllable. No one else can make you feel unhappy or angry. Only your own thoughts can do this. **You are totally in control of the thoughts that fire in your head -- if a bad one starts, you can redirect it.** Remember that thoughts are real things. They are physical. They are measurable. So your body can manifest a response to those thoughts in a physical reaction defined as a feeling.

Here comes the most powerful portion of this lesson: If your feelings are physical reactions to a thought and you have a non-conscious thought one of those you're not aware of, but that is firing at your non-conscious level, your non-conscious brain can send you a message through a feeling you get in your body.

It's important for you to understand that your feelings are physical reactions to your thoughts. If feelings (in your brain) are in response to your conscious thoughts, then feelings you have generated in your body may be a message regarding some thoughts from your non-conscious brain. **PAY ATTENTION!**

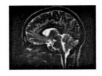

Brain Apples Implant #26: Talking promotes positive hormone release in the brain.

This implant is an excerpt from a book titled *Owner's Manual for the Brain* by Dr. Pierce Howard. I suggest that you check it out of the library and read it or, if you're really serious about changing, you may want to buy it, without being deterred by its cost and its size.

One of the things Dr. Howard talks about is the scientific evidence that the physical act of talking, alone, promotes a release of positive hormones in the brain. Of course, talking is a form of thinking. That in and of itself can release positive neurotransmitters in your brain, so there are two things that can come out of this knowledge. If you have a family member, an employee, a child, a student, an athlete, or an associate who has a problem or needs cheering up, **talk to them**. Just the fact that you engage them in conversation and get (or allow) them to talk, whether about that problem or any other event, can give them a release of positive neurotransmitters such as endorphins, which will reduce the transmission of pain impulses and generate feelings of pleasure.

How many times have you said, "I'm not going to talk to them, I don't know what I would say." In truth, it doesn't matter what you say. Just talking to them will make them feel better. So help your friends. Engage them in conversation if they're down, even if you don't think you know what to say.

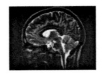

Brain Apples Implant #27: You can Lie your way to Success and Higher achievements.

I don't mean unethically lie. What I mean is you can *act* your way to success and higher achievements. In other words, if one of your goals is to be less shy, you can *act* less shy while you're achieving your goal. Remember that 5/6 of your brain takes every message you send it as real. If you send that message long enough (21+ days), adequate new DSP connections are formed so that your lie, or your act, or your faking will become your reality. Yes, this is lying to your non-conscious, but not in an unethical way. Let's call it "acting" instead.

So you can motivate yourself by acting like a motivated person. You don't know how to motivate yourself? Just pretend. Act like a motivated person would act. Guess what's going to happen? You'll become motivated! You can't help it. Your non-conscious brain can't tell the difference. That old phrase, "fake it till you make it," is pretty doggone scientifically based!

You use your conscious power to act like a motivated person, or you act like you are skilled in a particular area that is a goal of yours. That old cliché, "Fake it till you make it", has a scientific basis!

Whenever you stimulate your brain, it forms new DSP connections. 5/6 of your brain sees every image you generate as real. The new DSPs formed via your non-conscious brain, when repeated often, generate enough new connections to get the image onto your RAS important list (see *Brain Apples Blueprint System*). The DSPs will also get the image to influence your feelings, your attitudes, your beliefs, and ultimately your behavior—and then it turns to the truth and it's real!

Want to be successful?
ACT successfully!

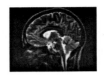

Brain Apples Implant #28: Worry is nothing more than negative visualizations.

My sister has always prided herself on being the family worrier. She does it for the entire family. But it isn't good for her health. A family doesn't need a full-time worrier. If you visualize what you do *not* want, you can give meaning to that statement at your conscious level. Your visualizations are firing in all 6 parts of your brain, are they not? If you visualize worry, 5/6 of your brain is going to take what you are visualizing as **real**.

If you want to be a high achiever, view high-achieving action patterns in your brain—advanced-achieving action patterns—not images and pictures of a negative:

> ➢ "I *do not* want to be ill on my birthday."

> ➢ "I *do not* want to get the flu this winter."

> ➢ "I hope my mother *does not* get that job."

> ➢ "I hope the plane my brother is flying on *does not* crash."

Worry is caused by negative visualizations, or manifestations of images as negative visualizations. What you need to do is redirect this habit away from those negative visualizations. Whenever you start to visualize a negative result, you can neutralize it by stopping at that point and turning the negative image into a positive picture, channeling your thoughts toward what you do want and taking a detour into the positive.

There has been study after study (a lot of them were not based in the field of neuroscience) indicating that the more you worry about an event taking place, the more likely that event is to take place. You can change the worry habit by redirecting your thought, by stepping outside yourself, as I have mentioned before, and noticing your thought patterns. When you recognize a negative visualization, whether for you or someone else:

1) Stop it in its tracks.

2) Do not just stop it and walk away. Stop it and turn it into a positive-positive picture. Instead of "Don't spill the milk," see the more positive, positive picture: "Hold that glass of milk with two hands and enjoy it right down to the bottom."

THIRTY DAYS OF THAT AND YOU ARE GOING TO ELIMINATE WORRY.

Do you know why we as human beings have such a tendency to worry? It is that doggone amygdala again. Human beings have had negative thoughts since being placed here by the Creator It is our birthright to overemphasize the negative. Don't think you have some defect because you "worry." It's not a defect unless you fail to recognize that you have total control over the emotion. Don't resign yourself to being "just a worrywart." You can change that if you want to by understanding one of the basic tenants of everything I teach. It's called IVM: **I**nner **V**oice **M**anagement. Using IVM, you come to the realization that the little voice in your head giving you negative input or negative visualizations is that doggone devil him, the amygdala, and sending negativity to your conscious level. Shut up that little deceitful voice. Change it, re-channel it to the positive, and worry can disappear for you. Not overnight. Not in 2 days. Not in 4 days. Not in a week. It takes a minimum of a month to change your brain.

I am reminded of an event that occurred a little over a year ago. At the end of January, American football teams competed in the Super Bowl. A few years ago, when the Super Bowl was being played, I was writing what used to be our flagship textbook system on achievement called *Mastery of Advanced Achievement*. In that book, I was talking about worry and negative visualizations. While I was writing, I took time out to watch the Super Bowl with some friends. It was a great game—the New England Patriots playing the Carolina Panthers—and it was a very close game. Near the end of the game, North Carolina scored a touchdown to tie the score.

There was a little over one minute left in the game, so if the kicker had kicked the ball, which is what usually happens after a touchdown, it would have gone deep into New England's territory. New England would have gotten the ball on their 15-25 yard line, which would have left them 75-80 yards away from being able to score points.

You know what happened? When the Carolina player kicked the ball, he kicked it out of bounds—a penalty that gives the opposing team the ball on their own 40-yard line, which made it a lot more likely that the Patriots would have enough time to get in range to win the game in the final few seconds.

I just bet you that right before the kicker went back onto the field while the television commercials were playing, he was approached by someone on the sidelines (a coach, a fan, another player, himself) who said, "Get a good kick there, Mr. Kicker, and *whatever you do, don't kick it out of bounds.*" That statement could have caused him to visualize a negative result. When he went onto the field, floating around in his head must have been negative visualizations—worry neuron connections that said, "Whatever you do, don't kick it out of bounds," because that is exactly what he did. New England, of course, took advantage of that kick, came down the field and scored to win the game in the final minute.

I would really like to find out whether that kicker is still playing football. I just wonder how many kickoffs he has knocked out of bounds since then. It would be very interesting to see if he went the next year without ever kicking a ball out of bounds again. When you visualize negative results, they become worry, and it is very possible that the neuron impulses firing at your non-conscious level will bring you EXACTLY what you worry about! **Worry is useless!**

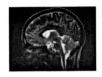

Brain Apples Implant #29: Intercept negative images and visualizations so they can't be completed.

If you recognize that you are forming a negative visualization, jump in front of it and intercept that ball so that it can't be completed, and then turn it into a positive. This is also one of our *Brain Apples Blueprint: Science for Success* techniques: "Stomping the ANTS (**A**utomatic **N**egative **T**houghts)." You have to learn to stomp the ANTS in their tracks and re-channel them into positives. If you start a negative visualization that will turn into worry, re-channel it into a positive picture by intercepting that negative pass. Do not allow your amygdala to complete negative visualizations.

hint: put a rubber band on your wrist for a few weeks and each time you start to worry or create a negative visualization, snap your wrist with the rubber band and turn that thought into a positive picture!

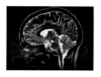

Brain Apples Implant #30: What is the definition of an optimist?

Years ago, when I practiced law in Ohio, I was a member of the Optimist Club. We repeated the worldwide Optimist's creed out loud at every meeting.

We certainly tried to maintain an optimistic attitude, but is an optimist—a person who is always optimistic, always happy, always in a great mood,-always looking at the bright side? No! Stop chastising yourself for not being an optimist. It's okay. Most visualizations or images of what we think an optimist should be are wrong anyway.

Here is my definition of an optimist: **An optimist is NOT a person who always thinks optimistically, but rather, an optimist is someone who knows how to intercept, interrupt and stomp negatives before they can get completed, and turns them into positive positives.**

Personally, I find it difficult to be around somebody who is flowery and bubbly and happy-go-lucky and looking for the silver lining all the time. Oh, hog manure. We can't act like that 24/7. What we *can* do is gain the skills to recognize a negative statement, visualization, thought or input in our brain and intercept it, interrupt it or stop it before it is completed, thereby turning it positive.

Want to be an optimist? Act like one. Consciously re-

79

channel your negative visualizations and thoughts into positives until they become habits.

Being optimistic is not something we are born with, but it is something we can learn. 30 days. 30 days. 30 days.

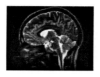

Brain Apples Implant #31: Evolution Pollution.

It is now known that our brain evolved to its current state from those humans who survived by overemphasizing the negative. Most of the neurons that fire in our brain come from the reptilian portion of our brain (sometimes called the limbic system), where automatic functions take place. The amygdala, that dirty devil, is located in your reptilian brain. The non-conscious thoughts that take place in the reptilian brain overemphasize the negative.

Negativity has been a brain habit for thousands of years. We are evolutionarily programmed for it. Early people on this planet survived because they prepared for the worst. It's not the same today. Our brain has not evolved in rhythm and time with the technological and cultural advances in our society.

Thousands and thousands of years ago, the overemphasis on the negative was a good thing, but it's no longer true. It is now pollution in our evolution. The good news is that you can redirect your brain's impulses. You can change the pathway your DSPs are taking and redirect the connections that take place in your new DSPs. You can channel and correct a negative thought that begins firing to a positive one.

You can change your brain's evolution.

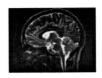

Brain Apples Implant #32: The human brain needs more light earlier in the day.

As we said in Implant #7, and in recent research studies, it has been discovered that students do better on exams in the morning if the rooms where they were taking those exams are well lit. This is one of those phenomena that we don't know yet WHY it's true but scientists saw the effects in several studies. Most of the subjects in the original studies were college students. Scientists then tested it again in middle schools and high schools with the same result. The students did better earlier in the day in rooms where there was better lighting.

Even without a science-based explanation, this is one of those facts we need to just take and run with. It just might raise you achievement levels 1 %, but that could be the per cent you need to reach the top! **Neurons fire better earlier in the day in a brightly lit room.**

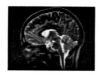

Brain Apples Implant #33: Stay fully hydrated!

Hydration has tremendous implications in many areas, particularly your level of achievement, your health, and your safety if you are working with dangerous equipment.

> *Don't be a half-wit! Drink Your Water!*

Scientists now know that, as a nerve impulse travels from brain cell to brain cell, it has to go across the synaptic gap, sometimes called the synaptic cleft. When two neurons connect, at the dendrite end (toward) of one and the axon end (away) of another, they never physically touch, so a gap is created. That gap is filled with a fluid that is mostly water, much as the brain itself is mostly water.

I remember teaching high-school science years ago when it was believed that what jumped across that synaptic gap was an electrical spark to carry the neuron impulse to the next brain cell. Scientists know that to be totally false now. Although there is electricity released in the brain—vibrations that are monitored as electrical in the brain—the action and reaction that take place at the synapse to carry a nerve impulse from one brain cell to the next is not electrical in nature; it's chemical. What's released across that synaptic gap is called **"neurotransmitters."** The process reminds me of a puff of pollen from a pine tree. When you shake a pine tree and a yellow smoke-like puff of pollen comes off. That is what this transmission of neurotransmitters across the synaptic gap does when a neuron impulse goes across that gap.

Scientists have found that, when neurons are released from one receptor, they move through that watery fluid to get to the receptors on the next neuron.

If you are just 5% dehydrated because you have been doing something without replenishing the water in your systems, including your brain system, doctors estimate that about 1/3 of the neuron impulse neurotransmitters don't successfully make the journey across the synaptic gap.

That means that about 1/3 of the neurotransmitters carrying your message to the next brain cell don't get through. If you are 10% dehydrated, up to 50% of the neurotransmitters don't successfully make that journey. If you are 5-10% dehydrated, your actions are based on only about half of the information your brain should have, and you are less coordinated and clumsier, and sometimes that can have disastrous implications.

It's important to understand the implications of this so you keep yourself fully hydrated at all times. **The connecting neuron process has several implications:**

1) Your balance is controlled from signals in your inner ear that go to your brain and then to your muscles. This is all automated in the reptilian portion of your brain 24 hours a day, 7 days a week, because you

are conscious that you must stay balanced so you don't fall over. If you are on a roof doing some work, it is, of course, important that all the signals relating to where your arms and legs are in relation to up and down, are firing correctly so you don't lose your balance or make uncoordinated movements that might result in injury.

All performances where physical movement is involved (including athletics) are included here. Your skilled movements, your quality movements, are influenced by the neuron-firing impulses that bring messages to the automated portions of your brain, your spinal cord and your muscles to keep you safe. You must stay fully hydrated so that every physical movement you make is based on all the available information in your brain and not just 1/2 of it or 2/3 of it.

2) To help you solve problems, resolve issues and face challenges. What mechanisms in your brain help you find a solution to a problem? I am about to give you a very elementary approach, but it should help you understand more about how this process works.

If you are faced with a challenge or something that needs a solution, you call on the memory storage areas of your brain to bring you information relative to that situation.

You might be making important decisions that affect your livelihood, the livelihoods of your employees, the safety of your friends, or the well-being of your family. If you are 5-10% dehydrated, you may very well be making decisions that are not based on all of the information you should have.

So how much water is that each day? There is no set formula or answer to that. The best answer I can give you is to always have convenient water within arm's reach 24/7, and always drink more water than you think you need, and do not just drink when you feel thirsty. By the time you feel thirsty, you are already past 10% levels of dehydration!

So drink some water!

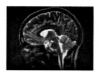

Brain Apples Implant #34: The 3% rule.

The effort difference between high achievers in athletics and high achievers in other endeavors, between the gold medal winners and the also-rans, is usually less than 3%! That is a very tiny difference.

That may be startling to you. I hope it is; it was to me. I thought the difference might be 40-50% when, in fact it's less than 3%! That's not much. But the percentage is about the same in all sports. The differences in the scores are in hundredths of a second or hundredths of a point.

I presume you are neither an Olympic contender nor a professional athlete, but this ratio also carries over into achievement levels of the rest of us, the average person in business, school, music and nonprofessional athletics. **The average difference between the effort, skill, knowledge, potential, etc., of those who win and those who don't is usually a difference of only about 3%.**

In terms of swimmers, for example, that works out to be a difference in preparation time each week of maybe 1½ hours, meaning that, if swimmers work out 6 days a week—a difference of about 15 minutes a day—they gain another 3-5% advantage. It's a very fine line. If there is anything you can do to give you an edge, no matter how slight, take that edge to the bank and use it.

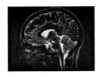

Brain Apples Implant #35: The amygdala is _Not_ your achievement friend.

As we said in Implant #10, when you are faced with a dangerous or stressful situation that is recognized by the amygdala, it will release hormones, or neurotransmitters, to bring you back to where you were, to calm you down, to give you strength, to keep you at your status quo. If you want to achieve more, however, the amygdala is not your achievement friend. But there is not a lot we can do about it. Or is there? Since fear is instinctive as a result of thousands of years of the amygdala's doing everything it can to keep us in the same safe environment, maybe we can change its instinctive behavior.

How? By consistently and constantly expanding your comfort zone to do things that you have never done before until the amygdala is comfortable with those things and recognizes those neuron patterns so they are no longer outside your comfort zone. **You should constantly stretch beyond the limits of what is comfortable to you, doing things that seem a bit crazy, to make you purposefully uncomfortable and out of your comfort zone.**

You will see this in our _Brain Apples Blueprint: Science for Success_ techniques. One of our new techniques is: "Get Weird to Get Wired," which encourages you to do something that you've never done before every single day. That action will intentionally tick off your amygdala and make it see those neuron patterns that are outside of your comfort zone so that, as each day goes by and you do more and more new things, those new behaviors will constantly be expanding your comfort zone.

Try to make the amygdala your friend by daily expanding your comfort zone. Your actions can be silly little things. They don't have to be big, huge steps or big goals. Get weird to get wired!

> ***Stretch beyond your limits ... Step out of your comfort zone!***

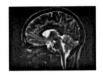

Brain Apples Implant #36: Always Be a Child.

By the time we are 40 years old, about 98% of the neuron connections (DSPs)—the connections between neurons across our synaptic gaps that carry impulses for creativity, visualization and imagination—have **atrophied** to the point where they are ineffective or have broken and separated the connections.

> **Rebuild Your Creativity and Imagination!**

When the cast comes off of someone who has been in it for a while, the muscles and size of the arm or leg have shrunk slightly from lack of use. That is atrophy!

If you don't use the connections in your brain regularly, or generate new connections for creativity, imagination and visualization, those connections will **atrophy** from lack of use! As a result, many adults have lost nearly all the connections in the brain that carry the impulses that perform those functions. This is frightening. Our culture somewhat discourages imagination and creativity beyond childhood, but don't fall victim to that idea.

Our ability to come up with solutions to problems depends on our power to use our imagination and be creative. **If you want to expand your comfort zone and level of achievement, you must have goals.** You must visualize, write, focus, refine, and be very specific with those goals. That's difficult, if not impossible, if you don't have the visualization connections. You must take steps as you approach 40 years old and beyond to create new connections in your brain for visualization, imagination and creativity.

You must reconnect with your creative and imaginative brain impulses. We now know that neurogenesis, the creation of new connections does occur, but that new growth of brain cells and connections requires an <u>active</u> effort on your part.

Turn on Your VCR (<u>V</u>isualization <u>C</u>reates <u>R</u>eality):

✓ Go back to your childhood and dream again. Fantasize again. It's fun! One of the favorite exercises in our seminars is our visualization/creativity exercise. It is amazing to me how exciting the seminar students become, and I think you can experience it too.

✓ Find a good passage of music without words. Listen to it for about 10-12 minutes. Then go back and listen again. Only this time, imagine and write out a story that seems to flow along with the changes in the music. This is great fun to read these stories. (Send me yours!) It is so exciting to regenerate and rekindle that interest in imagination, and it's extremely important to your ability to advance your achievements.

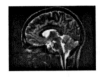

Brain Apples Implant #37: Pressure Points.

Pay special attention to this lesson if you have children you are a teacher or coach of young people, or if you attempt to motivate employees at work.

When you are under pressure -- in a pressure-packed situation -- either athletically or in business, the pressure causes stress to the neurons firing in your brain and, therefore, causes the amygdala to release neurotransmitters and hormones to save you from danger. **This will inevitably modify your actions.** It also requires you to concentrate on something other than what you might normally concentrate on in such a situation.

I'll use golf as an example, because my youngest son is now a golf professional. (He regularly shoots in the upper 60s, which if you are not familiar with golf, is really good). I asked him about stress when playing in a golf tournament or even just a friendly match with your buddies on the weekend. He said, "There is golf, Dad, and there is tournament golf, and they are different." I said, "What do you mean?"

"When you are just playing golf, the pressure—the stress—is not the same as when you are playing tournament golf and you are in a pressure-packed situation. It's entirely different. You take a different swing. You use different clubs." He went on to say that, in a pressure-packed golf tournament, if a certain club would normally send the ball 150 yards, that same club would send the ball 175 yards—12½% farther.

Why? Because the **amygdala recognizes the stress, interprets it as danger, and causes a release of epinephrine-adrenaline to increase the strength in the muscles.** When you are under pressure, your muscles have more strength than when you are not under pressure. If he attempts to make the same motion when he has uncharged strength in his muscles, his swing will not be nearly the same, will it?

So the lesson here is: when you are in a pressure situation, you may need to modify your physical movements or decision-making process.

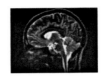

Brain Apples Implant #38: Think Execution-Pressure Points 2.

When you are in a pressure-packed situation, don't concentrate on the results you want. **Concentrate instead, on the procedure or the execution of the act.**

Remember, the amygdala overemphasizes the negative. It thinks it's doing that to protect you, so it may visualize negative results when you are under pressure. That might have been great a million years ago, but today it is not. Today, when you are under that pressure, don't concentrate on your results, as your amygdala may see them as what you don't want. Instead concentrate on your movements, your execution, your swing, your tempo, your rhythm, your form, etc., and you will see that you are getting tremendously better results.

When you are under pressure, the neurotransmitters being released cause your muscles to do more than you really want them to do in most situations that require refined motion. **You want to concentrate on the execution, not the result.**

Do not focus on the result or outcome. Don't concentrate on whether they will buy, whether you will close the sale, whether you will get the contract, whether you will get the job. **Concentrate on your**

effort, your presentation … the present action. The results will take care of themselves. But because the amygdala is so active when you are under pressure, it will do everything it can to make you visualize a negative result. Contrary to its own belief, it is not helping you.

As I said, my youngest son is a golf professional. When he faces a short putt (3-5 feet), it's a pressure putt. Why? Because he is absolutely supposed to make those putts. He rarely misses those so they generate pressure, because if he doesn't make it, it causes a strong negative that gets the amygdala going.

Back to the golf example … my son counteracts that pressure over short putts by concentrating on his rhythm or tempo, back and forth, back and forth. Not the RESULT! A little trick he devised is putting the rhythm of his stroke to the sound of the words "clickety-clack, clickety-clack." Back on clickety, forward on clack—the same rhythm every time with every putt, whether it is a short putt or a long putt. That forces him to concentrate on the execution because he is watching his rhythm instead of thinking about the ball's going in the hole or missing the hole, or looking up too soon and off-hitting or missing the ball. To this day, I can see his lips move when he putts. He doesn't say it out loud, but he does say it. "Clickety-clack, clickety-clack." He has not missed many 3-foot putts, I might add.

> *When you are under pressure, concentrate on the execution-not the result.*

95

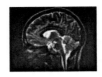

Brain Apples Implant #39: If others are doing it, don't. Go another way!

Most people are not high achievers, and you don't want to be in that category. 80-90% of our population, are not high achievers. If you want to be a high achiever, it makes sense to me that you look to see what others are doing in a similar situation, and then *don't do it*!

So, when you are deciding what action to take in any given task or achievement, observe and study what everyone else is doing and then do the opposite.

I don't think you should go directly the opposite way, but rather in a different direction. The opportunities for better results are there if you don't follow the crowd, because the crowd is not made of the highest achievers. The highest 3% of achievers is your goal.

> *The best results rarely come from following the crowd.*

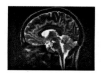

Brain Apples Implant #40: Create an environment of High Achievers.

If you're a parent, you may remember the teachers and psychologists saying, "If you really want to know what your child is like, look at their friends because likes attract?" Your children, my children, are as their friends are. If their friends are negative, you would want to direct them to more highly-evolved, positive achievers so they can visualize their actions/activities and form neuron connections related to those visualizations generated by watching the highest achievers. The same procedure will raise *your* level of achievement.

If you want to be a high achiever, surround yourself with high achievers. Create an environment of achievement around you.

- ✓ Befriend them. Put them in your mastermind group (many high achievers are very willing to join mastermind groups).

- ✓ Surround yourself with books that indicate high achievement, that tell you the story of successful people.

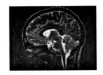

Brain Apples Implant #41: Surround yourself with an enriched learning environment.

In addition to circling yourself with high achievers, surround yourself with books that indicate high achievement, that tell you the story of successful people. Surround yourself with positive input. Create an enriched environment (television is *not* an enriched environment). The more enriched your environment, the more likely you are to form good neuron connections that mimic that enriched environment and become the basis for good actions on your part.

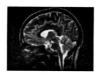

Brain Apples Implant #42: The Amazing power of Touch!

This is a very powerful Implant. But shhhhhh! It's a secret. Whatever you do don't tell your competition!

A research study being conducted at one institution is often mirrored at another institution. (If Stanford is conducting a certain type of research, that same investigation will be done somewhere else—maybe Harvard or Cambridge or Oxford—so credibility and statistical significance is added to both studies if the same results are obtained by different geographical locations and by different personnel using the same techniques, the same rules, the same applications.)

Case Study Example: Stanford and Cambridge Universities were both running a study about how well rats learn and how this **learning affected the physical size of the brain.** Could they show an increase of physical size in the brain as the rats learned?

Since they were doing exactly the same tests in California and England, using the same techniques and identical rats from the same supply house, they were shocked to see that the results were much different. They went back, looked at their notes and logs again, and reexamined the statistics and mathematical calculations. Still the results were different.

The brains of the Oxford rats were developing quicker, their weight gain from young to middle age (as far as a rat goes), was much better, and they appeared to be healthier than the Stanford rats. But no one could figure out why they couldn't attach any significance to any steps in the research study procedures that indicated why the rats developed their brain better in the English study than in the California study.

Then they found the answer: **maintenance.** When the California maintenance department cleaned the rat cages, they took the rats out and placed them in temporary cages. At Oxford, the rats were not placed into temporary cages during cleaning. They were held and stroked by some of the maintenance personnel while other maintenance personnel cleaned the cages. When the cleaning was finished, they put the rats back into their regular cages. That was the only difference in this study.

Touch stimulates the brain to form new connections and release neurotransmitters that generate feelings of pleasure and better, longer-lasting brain DSP connections.

This has far-reaching ramifications.

I also read a study about food servers that indicated that servers who occasionally touched their customers during a meal received on average, a tip over 30% higher than those food servers who did not touch their customers.

What an amazing discovery! **TOUCH STIMULATES THE BRAIN.** Use it with your children, associates and customers—with caution, of course, and with integrity.

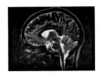

Brain Apples Implant #43: Study for an exam in 20 minute segments!

You have a **Hippocampus** in each of your brain's two hemispheres. Scientists have known for a long time that the hippocampus is somehow involved in memory. For many years, it was believed that *all* memory was stored in the hippocampus. That is no longer the belief, because we now know that the hippocampus is not large enough. It does increase in size, however, with increased learning and increased age. One of the reasons scientists used to think our memories were stored in the hippocampus was because it *does* increase. What they now believe is that the hippocampus temporarily stores information that you take in; then consolidates, organizes and categorizes that information; and then sends it to other areas of your brain for appropriate storage for better recall when you need that information again.

This has some tremendous implications if you study to learn new things, to take tests, to be licensed, etc. **What it says is: You must study new materials in short spurts—no more than 20 minutes at a time.** If you are studying new materials, study for only 20 minutes and take a break between each 20-minute segment. Even if the break is only a few moments, at least stand up, stretch and look out the window before you sit back down.

Why? Because the hippocampus requires time to consolidate and organize the information. If you don't give it a break every 20 minutes, it doesn't organize the information as efficiently as it could.

I know you can take in more than 20 minutes worth of information, but the hippocampus fills up quickly. (I know that college kids pull all-nighters, but that information is not nearly as well stored in the brain, neither is it as easily recalled.)

Stand up, walk around the room, and sit back down. It doesn't require a lot of time to clear the hippocampus and to consolidate and store the information. **Take 3 to 5 minute breaks** and incorporate some type of physical movement to help keep the blood flowing to your brain and help your hippocampus consolidate and properly organize the information.

> *Run wind-sprints with your brain, not a marathon!*

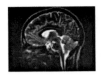

Brain Apples Implant #44: Study the hard stuff first!

Scientific research has also shown that you will retain the highest amount of information **in the first 5-7 minutes and the last 5-7 minutes of the 20-minute segment.** If you go beyond 20 minutes, your retention is greatly reduced from the beginning portion and the last portion. So study the hard stuff in the first 5-7 minutes and in the last 5-7 minutes of a 20-minute segment. Coast in the middle 5-7 minutes. You will be astounded at the increased level of retention. And, of course, if you have increased levels of retention, you are going to have increased levels of achievement.

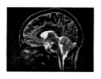

Brain Apples Implant #45: Subliminal sleep-learning tapes do not work!

A lot of people out there are selling CDs that you can play while you sleep to learn just about anything. These programs cost a lot of money, and people literally buy into the hype of it all.

Well, here is what the neuroscience researchers have found: **Any information you hear while you sleep does not go into the hippocampus nor is it consolidated, organized and retained.** When you are in a sleep state, impulses are rejected by the thalamus (it's like a mirror and bounces those impulses back). They are not absorbed; they are not retained.

The thalamus gland is what the scientists call the gateway or the gatekeeper for the cortex. All neuron impulses that come up through the reticular activating system, which we discussed earlier, on the way to the cortex pass through the thalamus. When you sleep, the cortex is busy. It is listening to itself, rewinding the day's activities, reviewing the events of the day, and any new impulses while this process is going on are bounced off the thalamus. They eventually stop firing.

So don't spend money on CDs that advertise you can learn a foreign language in just 7 hours of sleep. They just don't work!

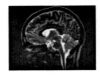

Brain Apples Implant #46: But, the good news is...

Scientists have discovered that the brain is most receptive to information and the formation of new DSPs, and your hippocampus is most capable of properly organizing, consolidating and storing information in the 20-30 minutes right *before* you fall asleep and the 20-30 minutes right *after* you wake up.

So the upshot of this is that, even though the subliminal CDs don't work while you are in a sleep state, you can listen to them as you start to fall asleep, or as soon as you open your eyes in the morning, the information is, in fact, better retained by the brain. I think that is one reason some people swear by subliminal sleep tapes even though they don't work during actual sleep.

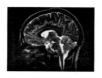

Brain Apples Implant #47: Make your own CDs!

Remember I said that studies indicate that subliminal messages don't work while you sleep, but are retained in the 20-30 minutes before and after the sleep state? Guess what? You really don't have to be listening subliminally during that period. That is a fantastic time period for **self-programming**.

I use the 20-30 minutes before I go to sleep to visualize my goals, my targets, my objectives, and my success scene. (Later in the *Brain Apples Blueprint*, I'll teach you some techniques for setting goals, visualizing your goals, and imagining having already achieved your goals--your success scene.)

Use that very precious and important time in a positive way and your achievements will start taking a quantum leap, because the neuron connections you are creating in those two 20-30 minute segments are nice, shiny and turbo-charged! They are the Ferraris of the brain cells—use them to your advantage.

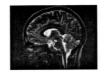

Brain Apples Implant #48: Reward yourself!

Reward yourself for little achievements on your way to the big ones. Shouldn't you wait until you get to the end and give yourself a great big reward? No. When you give yourself a reward, it establishes the psychological need for self-actualization. Remember that your non-conscious brain takes everything literally.

When you reward yourself for even tiny achievements, your amygdala orders the release of pleasure hormones, (neurotransmitters) like endorphins and dopamine, which reduce pain and also increase pleasure. Soon you become addicted to these pleasure feelings and you will want to repeat them again and again. **This is a good kind of addiction.**

If you reward yourself for the tiny steps and achievements instead of waiting until you get to the big one, **you reduce your risk of quitting**—one of the most common problems and challenges faced by people who want to reach the highest levels of success and achievement.

This habit is not something you have to force on yourself with willpower. Remember, willpower is only 1/6 of your brain's power—the conscious level—and that's not where your real power is. The power is in the non-conscious level. If you become addicted to pleasure feelings, they become automated neuron firings that will help automate your motivation, your achievement, your persistence, and your ability to overcome procrastination.

> **Little tiny rewards pay BIG dividends!**

Brain Apples Implant #49: Trust the darkness!

Remember the tragic tsunami in December 2004 in the Pacific? Many news stories that followed that tsunami indicated that certain cultures or groups of people sought higher ground just before the disaster struck. Most of the animals also sought higher ground, and very few animals were found in the debris after that disaster. These news stories said that the people and animals that moved to high ground had a "sixth sense," or an ability at the subconscious or non-conscious level, to know of the impending disaster.

There is no question in my mind that this "sixth sense" was a product of those people's non-conscious brain. As I mentioned in Implant #13, one of the *Brain Apples Blueprint: Science for Success* techniques is called "Trust the Darkness". This refers to the fact that you will get answers coming up to you from your non-conscious brain. Those answers may come in the form of ideas or picture patterns of something you should do, decisions you should make, or a direction you should go if you come to a fork in your path. **The "sixth sense" is the mechanism by which your non-conscious brain sends you solutions to problems based on your perfectly stored past memories.**

You probably can't recall everything that has happened to you in your lifetime. Actually, you shouldn't want to. I think that would be awful. One of the problems autistic children can have is that a sound or some other startling impulse that comes into their brain can start firing all their memory neuron patterns at the same time. What a horrible thing it must be for those children to have all of their memory images firing at once.

You see, many times the non-conscious brain speaks to us through physical feelings as opposed to patterns of images that we see consciously. We must be in tune and listening to our "sixth sense" (or hunch or intuition, as the news media likes to call it). Learn the basis for it and then you will certainly trust the darkness.

The lesson is to make sure your antenna is tuned to always listen for answers and suggestions—your gut feelings. It is very likely that the feelings are based on the most quality information you could get, because your non-conscious has access to all your past memories, even if you are not capable of calling them up to your conscious level. Our conscious brain is not our greatest power. Our greatest power for achievement is the non-conscious 5/6 of our brain, which allows us to use the "sixth sense."

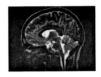

Brain Apples Implant #50: Top Secret!

This is one of the top three science-based secrets to success! Whatever you dwell on in your conscious brain, whatever your most dominant thoughts are at the conscious level, (don't forget that the brain sees in pictures—positive or negative—based on your thoughts.), **you must make absolutely certain that your conscious thoughts are firing positive-positive* images and not negative-positive* images because your non-conscious brain will act on those thoughts.** In other words, once the non-conscious brain is stimulated to fire its neuron patterns with the dominant thoughts that have been coming in from your conscious brain, it will go to work *automatically* to create pathways, new neuron connections, forward-designing solutions, and answers for those dominant thoughts.

These solutions, answers or ideas don't come to you just when you are seeking them. The ideas, the neuron pattern created by your non-conscious brain may suddenly pop onto your radar screen. You might be asleep, in the middle of a prayer or speech, watching TV, or even going to the bathroom. They may be a money-making idea for the Internet that comes to you while you're in the bathroom.

Unfortunately, sometimes we don't recognize those answers when they do come because our attitudes and/or perceptions get in the way.

The non-conscious brain always delivers a plan developed in response to our most dominant thoughts. The non-conscious brain is a genius in every one of us. We just have to develop the skills to recognize answers and solutions when they come. Our non-conscious genius works constantly and automatically. Unless we study it and recognize it, we take it for granted.

Think about this marvelous skill that you possess and how good it makes you feel. You can focus your attention on any subject you wish. You are in total control. By contemplating and thinking about that subject, you can always call up information and ideas that I define as genius. **That is one of the ultimate powers of a high-level achiever:** recognizing the power to trigger the unconscious mind into action by starting its motor and then recognizing the answers and solutions that come forth, and that they always will come forth! (Just not always on your time schedule.)

A positive-positive example is saying, "I eat only healthy foods!" A negative-positive would be saying, "I don't eat fatty food!" Both generate a positive result but the negative-positive creates a negative image in trying to get there. This will backfire! You brain will see: "Eat fatty foods!" Leave out the negative words!

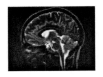

Brain Apples Implant #51: Get a digital voice recorder.

There is no option, and no alternative ... you must get a digital voice recorder. It would be a tragedy for you if you had ideas that you let get away. I would never forgive myself if I didn't insist that you have a way to create artificial long-term memory and then form the habits necessary to use it on a regular basis.

With my Olympus digital voice recorder, I can record and store up to 40 hours on the darn thing and then download it to my computer. You can often buy it for under $60 on the Internet. Just do a search for "digital voice recorders." Hundreds of websites and digital voice recorder options will pop up.

Record your ideas-before they disappear

On Sunday nights, I download everything I have put on my voice recorder from the prior week into my computer via a USB plug, so the audio file is always available. I can give them each a title and I can go to them at any time. I don't have to make my brain try to recall it from long-term storage. I have permanent long-term storage of every idea-thought I've ever had right there on my computer. I also now have software on my computer that can automatically turn the voice recording into text! *(I use Dragon Naturally Speaking, but IBM ViaVoice also has a good reputation.)*

If you have trained your brain to bring you money-making ideas, you need to record them before they go "poof" from your short-term memory!

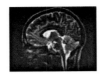

Brain Apples Implant #52: Voice recognition is a great author.

As I said in Implant #51, I can save the ideas and thoughts I have recorded on my digital voice recorder and turn them into written pages of text with *Dragon Naturally Speaking.* With its help, I have written six books. I have always said, "I am not a writer." I never thought I could do this, but once you know the power of your brain there is nothing you can't do.

Still, I don't really *write* my books; I speak them and my computer turns them into written text. This could be a great advantage for you if you own your own business or are in management. If you have sales calls that must be made, you can turn audio recordings into clauses for contracts or for estimating. If you are in the home-building field, you can use voice recording to do your estimating for you. **There are innumerable uses for a digital voice recorder and a voice recognition system.**

Your computer has to learn your voice and you tell it stories with your microphone. I read out loud until the recognition software got familiar with the inflection in my voice, the accent in my voice, the type of words I use. You can even add technical words to the list so it will recognize them. If you are in a profession that uses words not normally within a general vocabulary, it is a phenomenal tool. VR software will greatly enhance your achievements by giving you time to do other things.

(This convenience is not mandatory, but the digital voice recorder is. If you want to graduate from the Brain School, send me an email letting me know which software you got.)

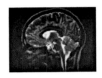

Brain Apples Implant #53: Strengthen your Corpus Callosum.

Your corpus callosum is the tissue in the brain that connects your left and right brains. In order for neurons that fire in your left brain to be transferred to the right brain, they must pass through the corpus callosum (and vice versa). You need to strengthen your corpus callosum for better thinking, better decision-making, better ideas, and greater achievements.

Why and how? That tissue between your left and right brain carries the neuron impulses from one side to the other. If you want a well-rounded, all-data-considered decision, grease up that corpus callosum. Do exercises to keep it firing well.

- One daily exercise is raising your right foot off the floor, whether you are sitting or standing, and make it go in a clockwise circle. Then move your right hand into the air in front of you and move it from left to right to form the number 6. See if you can keep your foot going clockwise as you make that 6 in a counter-clockwise motion. In general, women can do this better than men because women have a better-developed corpus callosum. Practice doing this two-sided exercise until you can do it easily with either foot.

- Another quick thing you can do is hold your nose with your right index finger and thumb. Then take your left hand underneath under your right hand and reach over and grab your right earlobe. Then switch to left finger and thumb and right hand underneath and touch your left ear lobe. Then switch back, and then switch back. Do this several times. What you are doing is forcing yourself to fire neurons across the corpus callosum, which will strengthen that tissue.

- Brush your teeth with your non-dominant hand, which makes you cross over and use the other side of your brain. You can shave with your non-dominant hand if you use an electric razor. (I would not suggest that you try this with a straight razor!)

- When you cross your arms in front of your lap like you are impatient. Notice what hand is on top, then attempt to cross your arms with the other hand on top.

Many books are listed on my website's annotated bibliography that have exercises for the brain to help you develop the tissue that interconnects both sides of your brain, the corpus callosum.

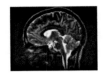

Brain Apples Implant # 54: Lose your mind.

You heard me right: Lose your mind. To me, your "mind" is your conscious brain. Your conscious brain is logical, rational, realistic and almost always wrong in how you perceive reality. Yet it does reason things out, which is why neuron impulses at that level take so much longer to travel their journey—up to 800 times longer than your non-conscious neurons. Your brain (as opposed to your "mind"), on the other hand, is the non-conscious (your noncon, subconscious, unconscious) portion of your cognition.

Your *mind* is your conscious thinking organ; your *brain* is your non-conscious thinker. Your non-conscious brain does exactly what you tell it to do, no questions asked. It does not add its own opinion, slant or interpretation like your conscious brain does.

The inner voice that is constantly talking to you, sending you messages, making you do things, and stopping you from completing new things is a product of the perceptions in your conscious mind. **So lose your *mind* and learn to listen to your *brain*!**

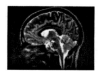

Brain Apples Implant #55: Laugh and have fun in all you do, even if you are faking it.

Put a sense of humor into everything you do, even if you don't feel like you are having fun and even if you don't feel like laughing. Doing so will change your mood at your non-conscious level and you will begin to have fun almost immediately. Remember, your non-conscious brain takes everything you send it—pictures, images, patterns of images—as real. So if you laugh, even if you are faking that laugh, it becomes real to your non-conscious brain and it will release neurotransmitters of pleasure and create stronger connections for anything you are learning while you laugh.

As doctors have always said, laughter is the best medicine, remember that old cliché? Scientists say so too. Research studies indicate that neurotransmitters of pleasure and thought patterns of pleasure and emotion in fakers are released just as they were in people who actually were having fun, feeling pleasure and laughing.

Fake it! Your brain will believe it and make you feel consistent with that act.

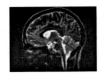

Brain Apples Implant #56: Change WHAT you think, not HOW you think.

It is not necessary to change the *way* you think or *how* you think. What is necessary in order to advance your achievements is to change *what* you think.

We have on the home page of our website: "Change your thoughts, change your brain, and change your life." If you change *what* you think, not the *way* you think, it will change your brain physically, measurably and physiologically. In turn, that change will change the neuron patterns stored in your non-conscious brain that formulate your beliefs; which will change what gets on your reticular activating system's important list; which will change what gets sent automatically to your conscious level upon which you act.

I am reminded of a student who took our course, "Mastering Advanced Achievement." One of the students' lessons is called "Mind for Goaled." They learn that they have to set goals because the brain acts on the goals you set. One of the goals for this student was to get up every morning and jog for 30 minutes. When he woke up, his inner voice would give him a hundred reasons not to run that day. He typically listened to his inner voice and wouldn't make himself get up and go. I don't think you have to *make* yourself get up and go. All you do have to do is make yourself say certain words that are consistent with what you want to do.

What I suggested to my student was very simple: *Put an index card on your nightstand containing the words you want your inner voice to say and the thoughts you want it to think when you get up in the morning.*

> It's the **What** not the **How** that matters!

I don't remember what words he put on the card, something to the effect of "I feel great this morning. I am so excited to take my morning run. I'm going to take my run now and have fun doing it!" When he woke up in the morning and his inner voice was telling him, "Oh, you feel like crap today. You didn't get much sleep. You have a lot to do," he would pick up that index card and read what he had written there out loud 4 or 5 times.

The first morning, the words got him up out of bed and inspired him to run. The second morning, it did not, and he called me and felt bad about that. I said, "Forget it. Do it again tomorrow, and then do it again the next day, and then do it again the next day," and he later said that, after six or seven days, he never missed again.

Change **what** you think and **what** words you speak.

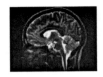

Brain Apples Implant #57: Never play <u>not</u> to lose. Always play <u>to</u> win.

If you enter a competition or you're a coach, never play or coach the game cautiously or with an attitude that says, "I'm trying *not* to lose this game." **Always coach or play to win.** There is a huge difference. Sometimes, when a team is way ahead at halftime, the coach will go into the locker room and change his strategy. He will tell his athletes to do things that indicate they are now trying to protect their lead. How many times have you heard that? "We were just trying to protect our lead."

> ### *Your words almost always control your actions.*

When you play the game *not to lose*, what you are telling 5/6 of your brain and 5/6 of the brains of every one of your athletes is a clear message of "don't lose the game." But you and the players will see the message "*Lose this game!*" If the image you are creating is "don't lose," you have a 5 out of 6 chance that you, your athletes, your players or your employees will lose the game!

Example: I do some work with a company in Orlando, Florida—call it the 4M Company—that works with professional football teams. One of the clients of the 4M Company who I have worked with extensively is Darrell Talley, formerly a linebacker for the Buffalo Bills in their Super Bowl years. He was an all-pro linebacker. Read his story...

The Buffalo Bills were playing the Houston Oilers in the playoffs when Warren Moon was a quarterback for Houston. In the first half, various things happened that were not expected but, as a result, at halftime the Houston Oilers were ahead of the Buffalo Bills 35-3, a seemingly insurmountable score.

When they went into the locker room at halftime, obviously the majority of his teammates were depressed and very little was said. It was apparent that they had developed a negative belief in the first half that they were going to lose. Darrell told me how, as co-captain, he went to his teammates one by one saying, "Don't you give up on me. Don't you quit on me. This is just the beginning. Yes, we didn't play well in that first half, but we don't want to be embarrassed. We want to perform at our highest level."

Now switch over to the other locker room. You have a team that is ahead 35-3. They obviously had a very good game plan going into the game to reach 35-3. At halftime, the coaches got together before they met with their athletes and changed their game plan. They discarded the plays they had diagrammed to use in this game. They got out of the files a sheet that would call more conservative plays by both defense and offense.

Disastrous decision, because then they went into the locker room and relayed to their team that they were going to change the game plan and the plays. "Here are the new plays we're going to use to protect our lead. We're not going to risk interceptions and fancy plays that might get the ball turned over. We are just going to play it close to the chest in an effort not to lose."

When they generated a picture of "not to lose" in the non-conscious brains of their athletes, what picture did they see? Lose!

*Believe it or not, Buffalo came back in the second half and won by a field goal, 38-35. All because Houston changed from **playing to win** to **playing not to lose,** and they got exactly the picture their non-conscious brains were creating.*

That doesn't mean that you don't teach your students, children or employees how to play a good defense. What you **don't do is give them images indicating that you are playing to make the least amount of mistakes so you don't have a chance of losing.** That is a negative positive, and you are more likely to lose if you do that.

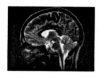

Brain Apples Implant #58: Don't <u>try</u> to change your life!

Here is a quote from one of my favorite books, *Think Like a Winner,* by Dr. Walter Doyle Staples: **"You can never change your life by *trying* to change your life. You can never change your performance by *trying* to change your performance. You can never change your behavior by *trying* to change your behavior."**

However, what you *can* change are the images, thoughts, internal representations and neuron patterns that you have created in your mind that represent your ingrained thinking, which are your beliefs and neuron patterns based on those beliefs. Those neuron patterns fire the most because they are based on the thoughts you most often think. The images you send in, the neuron patterns you create, the things that get put on to your RAS important list causes you to act in a certain way because those were your non-conscious beliefs.

1/6 versus 5/6. What's your potential?

How you perform in any given area of your life is only 1/6 a function of your potential or your conscious thoughts. 5/6 of your life is based on the neuron patterns that form your beliefs at your non-conscious level. How you perform in any given area of your life, no matter how badly you want it, how much potential you think you have, how much desire you have, how much willpower you have, 5/6 of the result is a function of the thinking you do with your non-conscious brain. Change your thoughts!

You can't change your life by trying to change your life. You change your life by changing your *thoughts*. You can't change your performance by trying to change your performance. You change your performance by changing your *thoughts*. You can't change your behavior by trying to change your behavior. You change your behavior by changing your *thoughts*.

> ***Change your thoughts, change your brain, and change your life, in <u>that</u> order.***

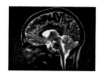

Brain Apples Implant #59: Some Brain Surgery homework!

Pass on this important implant to your children, your grandchildren, your employees, your coworkers, your students, and your athletes.

Here's your homework: Observe, with a scientific interest, statements of your friends and family when they are having a discussion with you about something that has been depressing them or a conflict they are having. Really listen to what they say. I have many good friends who sometimes rely on me for advice and comfort, and I am happy to share that. Close friends are one of the greatest gifts from God.

Has a friend ever said to you, "Ah, it's so hard. I have been trying so hard to quit smoking but I just can't change myself. I

> *Help others and you will help your own brain.*

have been trying to change my life but I've just have not been able to." **They don't know that they can't change their life by *trying* to change their life.** Be a good friend. Help them learn to change their thoughts and that will automatically, over time (not overnight), change their life—voluntarily or by forcing themselves, as we explained in Implant #2. Of course, if you help others, and you see them changing their life, that knowledge will generate the release of wonderful neurotransmitter feelings in you!

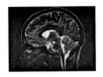

Brain Apples Implant #60: Turn up your mood.

In Implant #7, we told you about the study at the University of Pittsburgh Hospital where they determined, over a 30-month period, that the people in recovery rooms facing south needed 22% less pain medication because there was more light in their room. Now there is a new set of research from Harvard University: "New Scientific Era May Have Dawned for People with Depression" was the headline. **That depression fighter is called "light therapy."**

Research done at the request of the American Psychiatric Association concluded that daily exposure to bright light is as effective an antidepressant as drugs to quell Seasonal Affective Disorder (SAD), or cabin fever or winter depression, as it is sometimes called, and other forms of depression.

If you have "low feelings," they may be caused by thought patterns firing in your non-conscious brain that you may not even be aware of. If the light in your room is brighter, you are going to have an increase in more positive thought patterns at your non-conscious level, which will increase the quality of your moods and decrease the chances for depression.

Light therapy yielded substantial relief for patients with mild to moderate depression. Such therapy also magnified the depression-fighting effects of antidepressants in those individuals. Keep the lights turned up and you can take your achievements to the top!

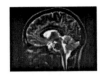

Brain Apples Implant #61: The Process of Visualization.

Visualization is forming abstract mental pictures in your imagination, i.e., using your brain to create, "see" and know. I am using the word "see" in quotation marks because the definition of seeing things in your imagination varies from person to person. I have occasionally gotten calls and emails from students saying, "I can't visualize. You talk about creating these vivid pictures in my brain, but I can't see those pictures."

One of the challenges with visualization is that when you can't see the house you want, for instance, you may be simply looking for your house on the inside of your eyelids. That's not what I mean by "seeing," visualizing and using your imagination. "Seeing" for some people may be the expression of words. Visualization for you may just be going through the process of telling yourself what the house looks like, whether it is two stories, what type of shingles are on the roof, or what type of windows it has.

> *Visualization is forming and creating abstract mental pictures or thoughts.*

Answering questions like those in words is the same as generating mental pictures. It's still the process of visualization—forming and creating abstract mental pictures or thoughts.

You may remember Bruce Jenner, an Olympic athlete for the United States. He won a gold medal in the 1976 Summer Olympics decathlon, setting a world record of 8,634 points. In his book, *Finding the Champion Within: A Step-by-Step Plan for Reaching Your Full Potential*, he says that, for the two years prior to the Olympics, it was a part of his training regimen every day to sit in an easy chair and relax and **visualize** every single aspect of winning the decathlon.

He visualized his participation in each of the 10 events every day. He visualized the playing of the national anthem as he accepted his gold medal on the winners' stand. He visualized and then, of course, he did win the decathlon. He did take that victory lap, carrying the American flag, exactly as he had visualized it for two years.

If you were sitting in the stadium watching a soccer match, the same neurons would be firing in your brain that would fire if you were watching and thinking about that match or even just imagining or visualizing that event. The same neurons, the same neurotransmitters, the same hormones are being released and used and, therefore, the same sensations, the same emotions, and the same neuron patterns are being called up. Whether in your conscious brain or in your powerful non-conscious brain, the same impulses are firing.

When you form new connections in your brain and are in a state of high emotion, those connections are stronger, and longer lasting, and they are more easily re-fired in the future!

Could you visualize your success in a particular category or event for two full years? Of course you could, and it would happen, whether you were working or giving a speech or sales pitch or writing a book, it would kick in. You would be forming new DSPs. The same result is created in the imagination as is created when you are attempting the real task.

Every time you send neurons firing down the same path, it becomes easier for them to go down that road in the future. **Use this to your tremendous advantage. If you have a tough presentation coming up at work next week, visualize it!** Go through it in your mind several times a day, every day, before your presentation and your performance *will* be better. **It's Do-it-Yourself brain surgery!**

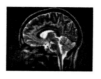

Brain Apples Implant #62: Learn a second language and be a translator!

No, I don't mean you should learn Spanish or French or German or Italian or anything like that. I mean you must **learn to speak the language of your brain**. I used to ridicule works not written by neuroscientists that claimed to know how the brain works and how people perform, react, respond and achieve. I thought that anything not based in the sciences was not worth looking at. I missed some very good things because I presumed, or assumed (and you know what happens when you *assume* something) that, because the book or report was not written by a neuroscientist, it could not be based in the sciences.

I have rethought that as I have grown and learned to achieve more and to be a greater success. I am not going to do that anymore. Here is my suggestion for you so you don't make the same mistake:

Learn to speak the language of brain science. Then learn to speak the language of the psychologists so you can translate their words into the language of brain science and apply it, using neuroscience techniques, to advance your achievements.

Jack Canfield is a good friend of mine. You have probably heard of him. Jack has sold over 100 million books as the coauthor of the *Chicken Soup for the Soul* series. Jack has written two books in the personal development arena: *The Power of Focus* and *The Success Principles*. I thank him very much for mentioning me and talking about what I am doing in *The Success Principles*.

One of the things Jack talks about in those books is *the Law of Attraction*, or The *Secret*.

The law of attraction is not a scientifically-based term or written in brain-science language. What Jack says is that **you will attract into your life what you think about.**

However, that is not what Jack meant at all. I needed to translate his idea into brain-science language to give it some significance for me since I believe you have to base your advanced achievement skills on the neurosciences and what the scientists have proven.

Now those same scientists have proven that the law of attraction works. Don't dismiss it. It is phenomenal. It is very powerful. I apologized to Jack for even questioning that the law of attraction works, because of what is it saying in scientific language. In psychology language, the law of attraction says you will attract into your life what you think about most.

What does that say in the scientific language? If you visualize your goals and repeat your goals in your Innerstates (affirmations) and your visual images, your thoughts will form new DSP connections in your brain. If you think about and visualize your goals when you are in a high emotional state, those new connections will be stronger, last longer and fire more easily. If you visualize your goals enough, the number of new DSPs will make your goal a belief in 5/6 of your brain, and it will place that goal on the important list of your Reticular Activating System (RAS). Soon this system becomes automated, and then, every time your non-conscious brain, through your eyes, your hearing or your other senses, comes across an image related to your goal, BAM! Instantly, it will call your conscious attention to it. It is automatic, as if you had attracted it to you. In reality it was there all along but you didn't notice it before!

After I bought a Chevrolet Tahoe SUV, I saw SUVs just like mine everywhere, as if by some "law of attraction" they were brought into my life. It was not a magical force at all, and it wasn't a law. It was science. A Chevy Tahoe was placed on the RAS's important list in my brain and, as a result, every time my non-conscious brain saw images of Chevy Tahoes, I would notice them at the conscious level. Did I consciously concentrate on looking for them? Absolutely not. It happened automatically.

It is wise to read some of the "nonscientific" studies on achievement and success, because there may be principles there that can be translated into science-based language that can be very helpful to you.

The Law of Attraction? "The Secret"? No! The more you fire neurons on a given topic, the more new DSP connections are formed, and the more often you repeat them, the more they will influence your beliefs.

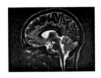

Brain Apples Implant #63: Read "The Success Principles."

Now that I have given you the basis for learning a second language, I am going to recommend a book to you. I couldn't recommend it to you until we had gotten at least halfway through this book and you had learned the language of the brain and recognized that the neurosciences can greatly advance your achievements.

Now that you know that, I am going to recommend Jack Canfield's book, *The Success Principles: How to Get from Where You Are to Where You Want to Be*. It's a thick book, and he worked on it for a long time. This book is not written in the language of the brain but, now that you have a tremendous amount of fundamental information about how your brain works, you can translate some of Jack's principles to what you now know about brain science and it will make sense to you. You'll clearly understand why you should do things in a certain way or why certain things happen. You have got to be a translator. If you can translate the book into scientific language, it can definitely help you.

(By the way, when you get Jack's wonderful book, whatever you do, do not go straight to Page 232 and read about me!)

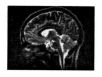

Brain Apples Implant #64: Sit up straight for smarts.

How many times did you hear your parents say, "Sit up straight"? Since the difference between high achievers and those who do not win medals is 3% on average, any little plus you can get is an advantage. Sitting up straight is one of those pluses.

If you are slouched, or hunched over with your head hung down, when you are working, thinking, studying, trying to learn what you are going to cover in your sales presentation, etc., blood flow to your brain is limited. If you limit the blood flow to your brain, it becomes short on energy and short on its ability to transfer all the neurotransmitters across the synaptic gap, just as if you were dehydrated.

Your brain needs nearly 30 times more blood than any other organ in your body. Anatomically, poor posture and slouching create crimps in the two main arteries that pass through the spine to your brain. Those crimps reduce blood flow (much like having a kink in your garden hose that cuts off the water supply). That reduced flow, of course, hinders thinking because it reduces the energy the brain needs to fully transmit all the neurotransmitters across the synaptic gaps. That will reduce your thinking ability and make your decisions less based on full information, which will reduce your mental performance and other cognitive functions.

Habitual poor posture is also problematic because, according to medical doctors, it can lead to mini-strokes—tiny, unnoticed strokes that damage brain tissue. If you suffer a mini-stroke, a tiny blood vessel in your brain has burst and the brain cells supplied by that blood will not be able to function. You must make good posture a habit!

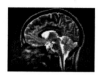

Brain Apples Implant #65: *Instant change? Not so fast, my friend!*

Put four stars beside this implant. "Instant" changes in your life, instant success, instant gratification in the brain, takes at least 30 days.

How long does change take using the science principles for advancing your achievements and the exercises we provide for you in the *Brain Apples Blueprint*? I have three scientific studies that clearly give an answer:

Dr. Richard Restak answers this in his book, *The New Brain*. Also, a study was done by Dr. Leslie Ungerlieder, chief of the Laboratory on the Brain and Cognition at the National Institute of Health,. And the third source is NASA, the National Aeronautical and Space Administration. All three conducted studies that concluded to make permanent changes in your brain that took about 30 days.

NASA did a study in which they placed goggles on some of their astronaut candidates with lenses that were convex and turned everything they saw upside down. If they were holding a glass, the contents of the glass appeared to be upside down. The astronaut subjects had to wear these goggles for at least 40 days. As they approached 30 days (I think the first one was on Day 24), the brains of every subject had formed enough new connections that their brains started seeing the images right side up, even though they were still wearing the goggles that turned everything upside down. After 24 days, one by one, the brains of each subject started to allow him or her to perceive things right side up again.

Conclusion: It takes, on average, 28-30 days to form enough new connections to make visual long-term changes in your brain. It is not going to happen overnight. It just won't happen that way.

Changing for success is not a get-rich-quick-instant-gratification process. If you want to make changes in your brain that will last a lifetime, give it a minimum of 30 days (preferably 90).

In the study by Dr. Leslie Ungerlieder for the National Institute of Health, it took 3-4 weeks before she could see changes in the activity patterns within the brains of the subjects.

Obviously there are some variations in the time it takes to develop new connections. It often depends on the amount of emotion involved when you are forming these new connections and creating these new tasks, but it is generally 28-30 days before any long-term change is observed and can be applied. There is no free lunch; 3-4 weeks, 28-30 days. If you don't have the willpower at the conscious level to do a task for four weeks before you quit, you can't be a permanent lifetime advanced achiever. Your brain will not make permanent changes short of that time, at least not by our own input. It may happen providentially, but we're not in that business. If you want to make permanent changes that can greatly advance your achievements, give yourself some time. Don't look for the quick fix.

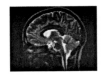

Brain Apples Implant #66: *Practice with conscious control*

Don't try to automate your skills for an activity too quickly. If you do so before you have perfected that action, it will be automatically turned over and performed by your non-conscious neuron patterns and you will not reach the highest level of performance for that action.

In other words, practice, but **practice with deliberate conscious control.** Don't turn the skill over to your non-conscious brain until you have perfected it. If you give it to your non-conscious too quickly, the skill will be limited to the highest level you obtained before you turned it over to your non-conscious brain, and you may not have perfected that ability yet.

As I mentioned several times, my youngest son is now a golf professional. When we moved to Orlando, he was 8 years old, and we joined the Academy of Golf at Grand Cypress Resort. In fact, I took a part-time job at the resort for the purpose of helping my son, who had set the goal to be a professional golfer. I'm not kidding—he did that at 9! We wanted to be able to play at a facility that had quality teaching and quality golf. Of course, one of the advantages of my working there was that we got to play for free. What a wonderful job!

A lot of professional golfers, and even people who were on the PGA or LPGA tour, came there over the winter to practice. One of the things we discussed with some of those professionals was how many golf balls they would hit from the practice range in a given day.

Corey Pavin is now getting up into his late 40s, but he was one of the best golfers on the tour in his prime. He won the U.S. Open golf tournament in 1995. Corey told me that he hit over 1,000 golf balls a day when he practiced.

Corey also told me something that, I now know, had a very strong basis in science. Corey said, "Yes. I hit 1,000 golf balls, but it would take me all day because I just would not, by rote memory, hit ball after ball after ball. I would take each individual ball and pretend and imagine it was a specific shot in a specific set of circumstances in a specific tournament that I needed a specific result from. That way, I had conscious control over each shot."

When you turn a behavior over to the automated portion of your brain, it will repeat the highest level of skill you have obtained to that point. If you have tried to perfect your golf swing (or whatever the skill is) by automating it too soon, you can't reach your highest level of achievement. Don't practice to the point that you become what they used to call at the Academy of Golf a "range rat," meaning that you just mindlessly hit shot after shot without any conscious control that would allow you to improve the action.

If you are having trouble with a particular complex performance, you may need to reopen your practice to the point where you go back in and form new neuron connections by using your conscious brain until you form enough new connections with the proper action and then turn it over to the automated portion of your brain. In other words, take in conscious control of your activity until you have refined it to the highest possible level and then automate it in your non-conscious brain, so those movements will be much more skillful. Practice deliberately.

You are never going to improve to your highest level if all you do in practice is hit shot after shot after shot—put a ball down, hit it. Put a ball down, and then hit it. If you don't take conscious control by visualizing the circumstances under which you want to make your movements, it certainly is going to increase your practice time. That is vitally important.

In baseball, in football, in soccer, in making a presentation, don't simply practice, practice, practice without taking conscious control of that practice so you can improve it. That's how you make changes—by being aware at the conscious level. Repeat the act enough times at the conscious level with the improvements you seek consciously, and then turn it over to your automated, non-conscious brain.

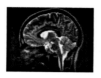

Brain Apples Implant #67: To prioritize, revisit March Madness.

I told you in Implant #9 that one of the ways you can overcome procrastination is to set up basketball tournament brackets and place everything in those brackets until you get down to the easiest task possible, and that you can almost complete that easiest task by just falling forward and accomplishing it because it won't take much energy. That will start your momentum.

One of the other things you can do with the basketball brackets is to determine your goal priorities. Many times, people have a difficult time getting their brain to help them prioritize their goals. If you have 6 or 8 or 12 or 16 goals and you're not sure which is your number-one goal, write them all on a sheet of paper and then tear up the sheet, throw the pieces into a hat, draw them out one at a time, put them on 12 brackets, and then decide which of the two that are matched up is a higher priority. Then go to the next round and do the same thing. Go to the next round and the highest priority keeps moving to the next bracket, and the other gets eliminated. By the time you get finished, you'll know what your top priority is. It's simple and works all the time. If you find other things you can do with your March Madness tournament brackets, send me an email and let me know what you use them for. I'll pass it on to everybody.

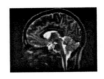

Brain Apples Implant #68: *Give yourself permission to play the game.*

Give yourself a ticket to get into the game via permission to want what you want. Many people don't give themselves permission to want even a little bit more than they currently have. They think, maybe based on neuron patterns that have been firing in their brain, maybe from their youth or upbringing or religion that they aren't entitled to ask for or desire more than they have. This is a very self-limiting set of neuron patterns that, if it is strong enough and it has been fired enough times, will become a belief that inhibits your actions to get what you really want. Give yourself permission at the non-conscious level to want what you want.

Put into your Innerstates (affirmations) and your goals, and into your synchronicity success scene, the permission to want them. You will never get anything you desire until you first, in your brain, form neuron connections that give you permission *to want*.

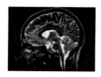

Brain Apples Implant #69: *Learn something new every day and never stop learning.*

On a daily basis, create new connections in your brain to increase your ability for achievement. Does that sound familiar? That is the very definition of "brain plasticity." What you are doing by adding new information to your brain, new things that you didn't know, will keep you learning.

Every day, put new DSP connections into your memory storage areas, because your non-conscious brain can call on everything in your database. The larger your database, the better your decisions will be. The better your decisions are, the better your solutions to a problem will be. The better your decisions and solutions, the more you will achieve.

Never stop learning. Read prolifically. Make a mental notch on your bedpost when you have completed the learning task so you form the habit of learning something new every day. What a phenomenally powerful, simple tool to increase your brain's ability to bring you better decisions, better solutions and higher achievements.

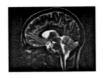

Brain Apples Implant #70: *Yes! Write it down!*

I know you have heard this idea before, but it has a strong scientific basis. If you write down your goals, the very act of moving your hand to put the ink on the page creates new DSP connections in your non-conscious brain that help indicate to your brain that this is something you want. It will help that written affirmation become a dominant thought. Remember, the main function of your non-conscious brain is to help you bring your dominant thoughts into reality. Anytime you have a goal, write it down, no matter how small it is or how large is, no matter how long it will take to achieve.

Writing your goals doesn't necessarily mean just putting words on a page, or typing them into a list in your computer.

Your goals could also be in pictures. About six years ago, my wife and I set a goal to be in our dream home by Christmas, 2004. We had pictures of it. I had a picture taped to my computer monitor and on my bedroom mirror. I had another picture of our dream home on the bookshelf next to my computer. I always saw it whether I was consciously looking at it or not. The neurons were going into the non-conscious brain if it was in my field of vision. That's the same as writing it down.

We moved into our dream home in November, 2004. I have to tell you, when we wrote down that goal, we had absolutely no means, nor any foreseeable way to obtain it. This story proves Jack Canfield's law of attraction and Doug Bench's scientific theory that if you generate a goal, your non-conscious brain will call things to your attention that are related to helping you reach it automatically. Less than 2½ years later, we had purchased that home and, in less than 3 years later, we were in that home. The only difference between this home and our vision was that the pond for the grandkids to fish in was out back. In our real house, the pond is in the *front* pasture, which is even better because we can sit on our second-story screened-in porch on the swing and watch our grandchildren play in the pasture, talk to the donkeys and horses, fish, and come running when they catch something. **Get three dimensional when writing down your goals. Don't just put them in words. Build a collage of pictures.** See, smell and touch your goal. Make it *specific* and in exact detail of what you *do* want!

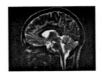

Brain Apples Implant #71: Burn this in with a laser scalpel!

During your next brain surgery, while you have your skull laid open for surgical improvement, be absolutely certain that you have the doctors burn this quote into your cerebral cortex and, more importantly, into your cerebellum!

It's from *The New Brain* by Dr Richard Restak (Pages 3-4):

"Brain Science is now capable of providing us with insights into the human brain that only a few years ago would have been considered the stuff of science fiction. We can now study the brain in real time and an exciting consequence follows from this study.

"Recent findings indicate that, by following certain brain research-based guidelines, ANYONE can achieve expert performance status in sports, business or academic pursuits! It is now clear that, by learning about this brain research and applying techniques based thereon, each of us can reasonably expect a lifetime of greatly enhanced personal levels of achievement!"

WOW! WOW! WOW!

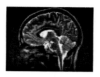

Brain Apples Implant #72: *Fail daily!*

From now on, go out of your way to be sure that you eagerly fail at something important every day. Then write down what you did and what you learned from it. So it will be a trigger to ensure that you grow from that failure. Sorry, not "failure." You can't possibly be a failure or have a failure or do a failure, but you can—and should—fail.

You can't learn or succeed better than by failing! That is how you learn.

Nobody in this world who has achieved high levels of success and achievement got there without failing time after time. The brain requires that you fail in order to achieve more. There is a portion of your brain that lights up in the frontal cortex when you fail. In that area of the brain, it is consolidating that "fail" information, preparing that "fail;" information, organizing that "fail" information, to come to a conclusion about the mistake made so that, when you perform that activity the next time, your non-conscious brain will send information up from the storage system to allow you to complete that task with better skill and better results. Fail as fast as you can.

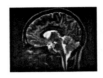

Brain Apples Implant #73**: **Tell at least two people that you love them every day.

NOTE: One of these must always be you!

Remember, 5/6 of your brain takes everything you send in, every picture, as real. If you don't like yourself yet or have no self-confidence, send love in anyway, because it is what's formed in your non-conscious brain that counts.

Send in love and respect because it induces positive, emotional neurotransmitters to be released. Even if you don't yet believe that you love yourself, your amygdala and your non-conscious brain can't tell the difference. The connections that are going to be created at your non-conscious level after you tell yourself that you love yourself will be filled with emotion and therefore stronger, longer lasting and easier to fire.

When you tell someone else you love them, you are doing two things: generating new neurotransmitter releases in your brain and making those people release neurotransmitters in their brains. Both of you have a feeling of pleasure.

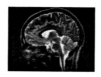

Brain Apples Implant #74: Procrastinators never took physics in school.

I believe that success gurus who say you should tackle the biggest problem first are wrong. Newton's Law of Physics says that a body at rest tends to stay at rest and bodies in motion tend to stay in motion. If you have a large mass to get moving, such as yourself, it takes a tremendous amount of energy to get it moving. Once you have it moving, it's hard to make it stop (that's the good part!).

If you had a tendency in the past toward that thing called "procrastination," break your choices down into the simplest, easiest steps you can possibly think of. Use the basketball brackets discussed in Implant #9 to prioritize until you get to the easiest step so that you can achieve it by falling forward, or you can't think of any reason not to do it. That will be your first building block toward momentum. If you have trouble with that little step, do something else. Anything. Sometimes, if even that tiny step toward your goal is too big for you, just take action by washing the car or taking out the garbage. Any action whatsoever will get your momentum going. I guess procrastinators never studied physics.

.

Procrastination is just a matter of physics. Once you get yourself in motion, it is wonderfully easy to keep that motor running with less fuel being burned to do so. Take little steps forward, even if they are not directly toward your goal. Eventually, you will start moving toward your goal.

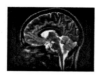

Brain Apples Implant #75: Never run a marathon!

In our *Brain Apples Blueprint*, I have a *Science for Success* technique called "Stomp the Ants". When you are in the process of conquering negative talk and replacing them with positive ones, you should never visualize running a marathon.

What if your goal *is* a marathon? What if your goal is huge? What if your goal takes a long time? What if you are running 26 miles to reach your goal?

Simple enough! Visualize running *one* mile 26 times. In other words, early on, as you are learning the *Science for Success* techniques, **as you are changing your brain one day at a time over the 100-day schedule for success, don't visualize your goal as the huge mountain or as the entire marathon that it is until you have completely re-channeled all your self-limiting beliefs at the non-conscious level.** Seeing the whole in this case will be counterproductive. The mountain will seem huge to you. Your non-conscious will not buy into it, but it will let you visualize running one mile, or 1/26, of your goal at a time.

Back in 1997, I made the decision to run the Disney Marathon—26 miles, 265 yards—in January 1998. I signed up because I knew I couldn't do it! I knew consciously that it was impossible for me to run 26 miles. I couldn't even run 4 blocks when I signed up, and that is exactly why I signed up. Do you understand that?

I signed up to raise money for the Leukemia Society, and they paid my entry fee and gave me a coach. It was a wonderful thing. Check it out at the Leukemia Society's web site (www.leukemia-lymphoma.org) if you have an interest. I had a very personal reason for raising the funds for the Leukemia Society: Two of my close family members suffered from cancer.

By the way, my first practice when I started training for the marathon was 30 minutes. I was not able to *run* for 30 straight minutes, so I walked and then ran, walked and then ran, walked and ran for 30 minutes. Eventually, I could see the goal of running 26 miles one mile at a time clearer and clearer. My goal was 4 hours; I crossed the finish line in 4 hours and 3 minutes. It was a wonderful experience. I raised over $22,000 for the Leukemia Society doing something I didn't even think I could do!

But I did NOT run a Marathon. I simply ran one mile 26 straight times!

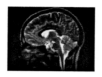

Brain Apples Implant #76: Visualization is 6-dimensional.

Visualization could be a misleading term, because it sounds like it means only what you see, as though it were only a visual experience. Some folks, don't see real images or patterns. They just *think* images or patterns. When you start to use visualization in our *Brain Apples Blueprint* techniques, you'll learn about 6-dimensional visualization and realize that visualization is more than just a sight experience. So let's call it "an imaginary experience." Or better yet, "Imagineering," as Disney does, because visualization is a full imaginary experience.

For you to have a complete and lasting impact on the neuron formations, the new DSPs, the new neuron connections, the new nerve patterns and the new neurons being created in your brain your imagineering should include much more than just seeing. It should include seeing, touching, feeling, smelling, moving, hearing, tasting, emotion, thoughts, and intuition. All of these should be involved in your experience.

Involving all your thoughts and senses gives you power. Focus on what you want down to the smallest detail— the handle on the kitchen cabinet, the upholstery in the car, the look on her face when you propose—everything about it. If you use your senses, the new connections in your brain will be much clearer to that powerful 5/6 of your brain, the non-conscious.

When my wife and I were working for our dream home, one of my favorite imagineerings was smelling food coming from the kitchen while my grandsons were out fishing in our pond visiting Grandma and Grandpa. My oldest grandson, Andrew, would come running toward the house from the pond and I could hear him yelling, "Grandpa! Grandpa! Grandpa!" As I heard the screen door slam, he came running into my study where I was working and said, "Grandpa, Grandpa, look at the fish I caught!" He was so proud of the pan fish or Bluegill that was about 5 inches long.

None of that was real. That was in my imagined visualization where I was dreaming in 6 dimensions about being in our new home and our grandchildren visiting. *But it's real now!*

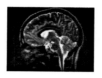

Brain Apples Implant #77: The "how" comes later.

Keep in mind that it is not necessary to create your "how" before you start dreaming and visualizing in 6 dimensions about your goals. Don't get the cart before the horse. You don't need to worry about the means. The means, the "how", will show up once you have developed the goals and have visualized on a regular basis. Your brain will bring you the answers. Your emotion will create strong connections. Your non-conscious brain will soon get the message that the goal goes on your important list, and it will send you every impulse it notices relative to getting that goal.

We teach you in The *Brain Apples Blueprint* that you need to "trust the darkness" (see Implant #13). It will bring you the solution. You don't have to fit and fuss over not knowing how you are going to do it.

Let me give you an example: *In December 1994, my two oldest grandsons, who were the only grandsons I had at the time, came down with Strep throat. I had always gone up to Atlanta to see them at Christmas. How awful it was that, at age 3½ and 6½, they had Strep throat for the holidays. As their grandpa, I set a goal to make an additional $5,000 or more through my websites between December 17th and the end of December so I could do something special for my grandsons when they got well from their Strep throat.*

I had no clue how I was going to make that $5,000 when I set that goal, but it didn't matter. All I did was set the goal and start visualizing things I was going to do for my grandsons to make it up to them that they had to be sick over the holidays. What I set up was for them to come to Disney World and have breakfast with Mickey Mouse and to have backstage passes for a lot of the things in Disney so they could have a phenomenal experience! Well, okay, maybe that's a little indulgent, but my job as grandpa is to spoil those boys!

I set the goal. I started visualizing in 6 dimensions. I started imagineering that goal and my non-conscious brain brought me an idea for something to add to two of my websites that brought me, in a week, almost $11,000 in additional revenue. I set that goal knowing I didn't know how it was going to happen. Thank you, non-conscious brain!

You don't have to know the "how" to go ahead and set your goals and visualize them. Your non-conscious brain will never fail you as long as you put the right things in and pay attention. It will always bring you the solution. The "how" will come later, **every time**.

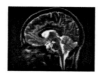

Brain Apples Implant #78: The language of your non-conscious brain is body language.

Since you are now consciously aware of what your non-conscious brain is thinking, the only way it, under most circumstances, can originate a communication that it needs to get to you is by body feelings. The language of your non-conscious brain is the feelings you sense at the physical level.

Sometimes we search so hard for an answer, a solution, or a message that we miss the communication being sent to us by our non-conscious brain through our physical feelings. Sometimes the only way it can get messages through, because we are trying so hard to find the message, is through our body. You must be very sensitive when your body is talking to you. You must be aware of it, acknowledge it and tune into it

One of the ways I learned that my non-conscious brain spoke to me through my body was when I was training for the Disney marathon. Sometimes I would go out on a Sunday morning or evening for my long (often 14 miles) run, and some days I wouldn't get two blocks from the house before I was huffing and puffing. At that point, my non-conscious would send me a message through my body: "You should stop. I am going to make your knee hurt. I don't want to do this today. This is painful. You can't run 14 miles. I am going to send a pain to your side so you will stop."

I would talk back to my non-conscious brain and say, "Shut up! I'm not listening. We are going 14 miles. I know you're faking that injury to my knee. I know those feelings are not real. I know what you're trying to do. We are going 14 miles, so shut up! Oh, I will let you play around for another quarter of a mile but then settle down because you have too much work to do to be sending me these messages. Send me the good stuff."

I got a little carried away there, but the point is that the pain/thought of quitting would *always* go away after 15 minutes or so.

You have to be aware that your non-conscious brain can talk to you through your body. Sometimes what it is saying to you is not the truth, but it is a feeling you get. ***Your amygdala does lie to you!*** Sometimes it's a feeling of a flushed face or a cramp in your leg or a chest pain. Be aware of it. Be alert to it and be listening for it.

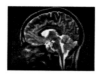

Brain Apples Implant #79: *Thoughts are real things.*

If you have not formed a belief about the power of your non-conscious by now, listen to this! Brand new research proves that **thoughts are real things**, that they can be seen in the brain and that you have a non-conscious brain that does thinking that you are not even aware of at the conscious level.

A study released from the University College in London indicates that **a brain scan can read brain activity from the non-conscious neuron patterns stored in a person's non-conscious brain**, even though the person being scanned could not consciously recall those thoughts.

Here is what happened: *Researchers placed some subjects into a functional MRI (Magnetic Resonant Imaging) scanner. MRIs are frequently used to monitor brain activity by mapping blood flow in different parts of the brain. The researchers flashed pictures onto a screen of different shaped images and observed the functional MRI scans of the subjects so they could distinguish which shaped image the person had seen with their non-conscious neurons, even though the subjects were not consciously aware that they had seen that card. Did you follow that? For example, a square, a circle, a rectangle or a triangle would flash on a screen at a speed so fast that a conscious brain could not even see it, but the researchers could do a functional MRI of the seer's brain and tell with 100% accuracy which picture shape had been seen. Do you remember when I said that the non-conscious brain sees about 800 times faster than the conscious brain?*

There is another a new study published in the journal Nature: Neuro-Science. The researchers were Dr. Geraint Rees and Dr. John-Dylan Haynes. This study confirmed that, by looking at the brain scan of an individual, researchers could tell what shape of object the person had seen.

Another neuroscientist, Dr. Adrian Burgess, has proven that your non-conscious brain is thinking thoughts of which you are not consciously aware!

Conclusion: You have a subconscious, non-conscious brain. It thinks thoughts that you are not consciously aware of. The potential for this in the future is powerful. It can potentially be used to discover the latent attitudes and beliefs that are holding you back. This is a scientific way to do what we are going to teach you in the *Brain Apples Blueprint* technique called "Synchronicity," where we tell you how to feel and be aware of what your non-conscious thoughts are so that you can get them in synch with your conscious brain. It is a long, hard process, but it's amazingly powerful!

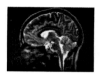

Brain Apples Implant #80: Exercise in any form is brain food.

Many studies have shown the benefits of physical exercise on certain psychological areas. Exercise can be used to treat depression. It will reduce stress, which will make you healthier. But can exercise in and of itself affect raw thinking power—your capacity to think or plan or learn or achieve? There are now studies supporting that exercise will improve your level of cognitive achievement. There have been some intriguing findings just recently published demonstrating that exercising for 30 minutes per day, 5 days a week, results in an increase in cognitive skills as well.

Humans need to exercise continuously for at least 30 minutes for 5 days a week and, for your brain and body, you need to vary that exercise. Walking is certainly the best exercise for your brain, but you must vary your exercise for other aspects of your training and brain. Studies at the University of Illinois and others in mirrored research proved, through the neurochemical and neurocellular changes in a brain, that aerobic exercise promotes the development of new DSP connections and increases the flow of neurotransmitters. Enhanced cognitive functioning! Even if you previously were a stick-on-the-couch potato, get up and exercise 5 days a week, 30 minutes a day, for 30 days and you will start to increase your cognitive functioning.

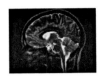

Brain Apples Implant #81: To reduce your pain, overload your brain.

I just heard on the news that over 50 million people in the United States suffer from chronic pain. Over 50% of all working Americans suffer some back pain symptoms each year. 80% of Americans are *expected* to experience back pain during their lives. This, of course, has a tremendous impact on the amount of money spent for medical care; doctors are estimating that people will spend over 50 billion dollars a year to neutralize that pain with medical treatment and medications.

Here's what they <u>didn't</u> say: **If you over-stimulate your brain by sending in impulses, the perception of pain will be reduced.** This too has been proven by scientific studies and was the theory for my Master's thesis and research study way back in 1969 at the University of Toledo.

My research study showed that if you greatly increase the input of stimuli to the brain from senses other than pain receptors, it will cloud the brain's ability to interpret the pain impulses. Of course, in 1969, we had no way of knowing whether this was true or not, or how it worked, because there was no brain-imaging equipment available. It was just a theory I had that if you overload the brain with a certain type of stimuli, it can't pay much attention to other types of stimuli.

At that time, I ran some experiments on college and high school students. They exercised to physical exhaustion while listening to headphones. One group listened to white sound, which is the sound of static or rushing water or Niagara Falls. The second group listened to very loud music, and the third group had on headphones but listened to nothing.

I discovered from my research that the group listening to white sound could exercise about 17% longer before they reached physical exhaustion than either of the other two groups (10-11% longer than the group that listened to nothing). My thesis inferred that the sound impulses were making it more difficult for the exerciser's brain to interpret the pain impulses, so they didn't feel as much pain. When we exercise to the point of total exhaustion and collapse, the collapse is usually not physical—it is mental.

Although my study was published by the University of Oregon Press as a significant study, it was not taken as gospel because it was only significant to the .05 level, meaning there was a 5% chance that the findings were discovered by chance and not by the scientific conclusion we reached.

Today, some 40 years later, scientists and doctors are discovering, that if you distract the brain with an overload of impulses (visual stimulation, audio stimulation, smell stimulation or thought stimulation) the amount of pain a person feels is significantly reduced.

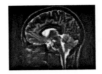

Brain Apples Implant #82: Self-help doesn't!

The vast majority of self-help exercises, self-help gurus, self-help books, and self-help CDs don't help. You can't make permanent changes in your life without making permanent changes in your brain. You can't make permanent changes in your brain overnight by memorizing one article, reading one book, or listening to one CD. **You can't make permanent changes in your brain that quickly. The only person who can make those kinds of changes in the brain is the Creator.**

For the rest of us, it takes at least 28-30 days of changing your thoughts before you can change your brain and change your life. Most self-help gurus, don't even give you a solution, let alone tell you that to implement a solution takes a 30-day period of repeated change of thoughts. You have to understand that self-help doesn't usually help unless it is science-based. And all science-based help takes time!

I think about the neuroscientists. I think about the brain, and I think about the scientifically-proven facts that you can't make permanent changes in your life by trying to change your *life*. The only way you can do it is by changing your thoughts, which takes a minimum of 28-30 days of constant, sweaty, struggling effort. Then you have a maintenance period that lasts forever.

Many times, I have said to people in my audience, "Please raise your hand if you have been helped by positive thinking." Hardly ever does a hand go up. That's too bad. No, that's tragic. The only way you can help yourself is to change your thoughts. Understand that you have to change them and work on them for 30-120 days before the change will be permanent.

> ### *There's no quick fix for your brain!*

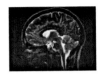

Brain Apples Implant #83: *Send your brain to the bank.*

One of the things the Salk Institute in La Jolla, California, is answering with their research is not whether new brain cells will grow if you exercise and stimulate your brain. Now the question is more under what conditions and where the cells will grow. You don't get *just* increased cognitive function, achievement and success by exercising. Exercising, particularly walking or running, on a regular basis also will help slow down the aging process and possibly prevent or delay the onset of degenerative diseases such as Alzheimer's and memory loss.

So not only is exercise tremendous brain food to increase your cognitive function, it may very well create a **neural reserve** buildup so that, if you had some brain cells degenerate due to Alzheimer's or aging or other causes, these new neurons could be substituted for those brain cells that were dying off or degenerating.

What a fantastic concept! Send your new brain cells to a bank to be withdrawn later as needed for your retirement. Are you getting the picture that physical **exercise is vital for maintaining good brain health and achievement skills?**

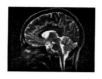

Brain Apples Implant #84: *For adults only! X-rated!*

Staying on the theme of exercise and the brain, I have some tremendous news for everyone! Solving crossword puzzles, playing cards, doing Sudoku puzzles, etc., are all a form of exercise that stimulates your brain. **But one of the BEST forms of exercise is sex! Sex can be used as a tool to increase your cognitive function abilities.** Yahoo!

(Caution: This Brain Implant should only be used by consenting adults!)

\

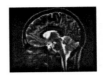

Brain Apples Implant #85: All new scientific discoveries are first the subject of ridicule and rejection.

It has been shown that a new scientific discovery is first treated with disdain. Dr. Restak says in *The New Brain* that new science discoveries take 9-12 years before they are accepted as the norm. For the first 3-4 years, a scientific discovery is usually treated with cynicism or rejected. For the next 3-4 years, it's treated with caution and skepticism. It usually takes another 3-4 years before the discovery is accepted and goes into the mainstream.

You can be 9-12 years ahead of your competition if you take all these science lessons and discoveries in this book and apply them *now*. Don't wait the 9-12 years, implement them **now**. The fact that you may think some of them are hokey is exactly why you should accept them now and **get ahead of your competition!**

When you get out ahead of your competition, when you get out ahead of everybody on the other team and you see the goal line, *don't* look back. They're comin'! You don't need to look and see. They're comin'!"

If you look back, it's going to slow you down. Implement these ideas NOW!

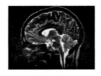

Brain Apples Implant #86: Working hard no longer works.

Working hard no longer works? I have to tell you that this is one lesson that has been very difficult for me to accept. It is no longer true in our culture that the harder you physically work, the more money you will make. That was true in the 1800s and early 1900s, and even up through the mid 1980s in this nation. And I'm sure it was true in other cultures as well. The harder you physically worked, the more you sweated, the longer hours you put in, the more income you would generate. Today, is the end of the era of "carrying buckets." Once upon a time, the more buckets of water you carried down to the village for the village people, the more money you made. If you wanted to make twice as much money, you carried twice as many buckets. That is no longer true.

You don't need to work *harder* to make more money. You need to work *smarter* and *better* to make more money. You need to train your brain for permanent self-motivation skills; for money-making ideas; for success! You need to train your brain to get the best out of your employees. You need to train your brain for success.

Today, you stand on top of the mountain and **devise ways to train your brain** to bring you an idea to get that water to the people in the village without carrying the buckets. You think it through. You train your brain for 30 days or more, and you devise a way to take a pipeline down to the village and put a meter on that pipeline and measure the flow of the water through that pipeline so you can bill people each month for the water they use and let you kids use your buckets to plant flowers!

Brain Apples Implant #87: Don't be a pain in the butt.

Have you ever heard the expression "you are a pain in the ass"? Of course you have! So have I... many times. But the truth is that pain is not located in the ass. So there!

Pain originates in the brain. Stimuli that appear to cause pain in your foot, in your leg, in your behind, in your hand, in your back actually are perceived in the brain as impulses.

Pain, chronic pain in particular, can shrink your brain, or at least the number of neurons you have in your cortex. The conclusion from this discovery is that, if you suffer from chronic pain, in particular chronic back pain, that pain will influence a substantial amount of impulses in your brain. These are the neurons usually used for other functions, and they will atrophy as a result of your pain and decrease that area of the brain's ability to process information.

The good news is that pain is not in your butt or your back. Pain is in the brain. Brain research being conducted at the University of Michigan indicates that pain is probably not a symptom itself, but is a non-physiological disease located within your brain. MRI evidence indicates that pain is located in your brain—and only in your brain. You may perceive that those symptoms are in your arm, your leg, your back, your knee or your behind but, in reality, they are located in the brain. Pain is an illusion and, therefore, can be changed by creating another illusion in your brain.

Phantom pain results, or is perceived to result, when a hand, arm or leg has been amputated. In other words, some subjects who have had a limb removed through a traumatic incident or because of surgery have indicated that they still felt severe pain in the limb even though it was no longer there. They absolutely, positively indicated that they felt pain. Some of the subjects, for example, even indicated that they could tell when their hand was swollen because their ring finger was hurting under their wedding ring—even though their ring finger (and hand) was no longer there.

Researchers took subjects who were suffering from phantom pain and placed them in an apparatus called a "mirror box." When viewing their good limb—the one that was really there—in that box, a reflection of the good limb was created that made it appear as if they now had two good limbs in front of them. The mirror image of their right arm and hand, let's say, on the left side, which was really merely a mirror image of the right hand, made it look like they also had a left hand. The only thing missing was the wedding ring on that hand, of course, unless you put one on the right hand and it showed up in the mirror on the left.

The doctors had these patients look at the image of their phantom limb, so to speak, in the mirror on the left side and their real limb on the right side. For a period of— guess how long—3-4 weeks, the patients did exercises with their good limb while looking at "both" limbs in the mirror image, 3 times a day, 15 minutes minimum. After 3-4 weeks, all the phantom pain disappeared completely!

What is the conclusion? These patients created the illusion that they still had two good limbs. There is no longer any reason for their brain to fire the pain impulses because they have successfully convinced 5/6 of their brain, the non-conscious brain, that there are two good arms there. Why create pain if you now have two good arms just like you used to? Remember, the non-conscious brain can't tell the difference between real and imagined, truth and a lie, and every picture you send it is taken as real. After 3-4 weeks, you will build up enough new DSP connections, to take that illusion and turn it into a reality.

And, of course in this research, they had control groups that were suffering phantom pain and had them exercise with their good limb for 3-4 weeks, but without the mirror box so there was no picture or image or illusion for them of a second limb. Those folks did not lose their phantom pain.

This is scientific data that may help many people. Obviously, your brain can influence your achievement and your success. You may be able to control, or even eliminate, your pain by creating the illusion in your brain for a 3-4 week period. The way you use your brain has everything to do with everything you do! The power of the brain is phenomenal!

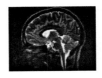

Brain Apples Implant #88: Be careful what you wish for!

Dr. Tanya Chartrand, of Ohio State University, through her research determined that your non-conscious brain can form goals for you of which you are not even consciously aware, because of the input that goes into your brain. (You should know by now how vitally important self-talk is and be aware of what you are saying to yourself.)

Dr. Chartrand discovered that, if you fail to reach that goal you didn't even know about, it can greatly influence your attitude, moods and feelings. **Remember, your non-conscious brain talks to you through physical feelings.**

Dr. Chartrand had a group of subjects come in for testing. She lied to them for the purposes of this test and told them that she was measuring how well their brain could recall information and whether that correlated with their manual dexterity. In other words, if you are good with solving puzzles with your hands, do you have a better memory? But that's not what she was really testing.

Dr. Chartrand gave one group a list of words and asked them to read the list over and over on a daily basis, 2-3 times a day for 3-4 weeks. Then she had them, each day, attempt to solve a manual dexterity puzzle with their hands—one of these wooden puzzles that you can take apart and put back together. She was going to measure how long it took them to take apart and put back together the puzzle. But in reality, the puzzle was not solvable—it was impossible to take it apart and put it back together. Of course, she didn't tell them this.

She gave words to the first group of subjects that were indicative of, or implied, being successful—words such as success, achievement, fulfillment, graduation, reward. The second group of subjects had random words with no pattern or relationship to each other. Then, of course, she had a control group that did not memorize words at all, but attempted to solve the puzzle.

She found, after the 3-4 week process of measuring the moods, feelings and attitudes of the subjects, and 90 days after the process, that the subjects who were given the achievement-oriented words to memorize remained in poorer moods about everything, as measured on her scale, than the group that had random words and the group that had no words at all.

Conclusion: The non-conscious brains of the subjects who were in the group that had repeated the words related to achievement and success were forming new DSP connections in their brain related to those words, so their non-conscious brain inferred that it was imperative to solve the puzzle. When they were unable to solve it, the non-conscious brain sent negative feelings and attitudes because it had failed at what it had taken as a directive. Notice what you are saying to yourself!

The important thing to note in her research is that you have to pay attention to your self-talk because you may be setting goals for yourself that are outside of your awareness and conscious intent and, therefore, outside of your conscious control. And those "invisible" goals may influence your behavior, your moods and your beliefs about yourself as well as others.

> **If you repeat negative statements, you will generate negative goals AND NOT KNOW IT!**

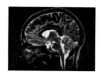

Brain Apples Implant # 89: Stress is the enemy to your body and brain.

Stress is a related source of at least 70% of all illnesses. In and of itself, stress is caused by what? Tension, anxiety and all those psychology terms? No. Stress in the brain is caused by negative visualization.

If you change those negative visualizations, you can eliminate the stress. When you have negative visualizations, toxins are released in the brain. If they are not cleared, they flow through the blood stream into the body and can generate physically manifested illnesses. Eliminate stress and you can nearly eliminate your risk of illness.

How do you eliminate stress? By stomping out those negative visualizations. But don't just stop them; you must change the course of those negative thoughts and visualizations that are creating stress and turn them into positive positives. The energy used to turn them into positive positives can be totally unrelated to the issue causing the stress. Your stress may be in reference to a negative visualization, perhaps the fear that you are going to be fired in the next week. You can take that negative thought and turn it into a positive about something you want to accomplish in your kitchen. It makes no difference if they are related so long as you complete the thought as a positive one.

The second thing of importance about stress is that there is now scientific evidence that stress makes you more forgetful. Stress can keep neuron impulses from going into long-term memory storage. The brain can't store energy so, as a result, when the brain is firing neuron impulses, those impulses are first placed in short-term memory. And to get thoughts and neuron patterns into long-term memory requires some action on your part.

Stress inhibits the performance of an action so that memories currently in short-term memory, or working memory, don't get transferred to long-term memory before they stop firing in short-term memory. If that happens, you won't be able to recall that neuron pattern. So stress not only can cause illness, but also forgetfulness and memory loss. So we have to back up and learn to stomp out those negative visualizations that are creating that manifestation we call stress.

How do you do that? The first step is what we mentioned before: Stomp the automatic negative thoughts.

Another way is to fake it. Pretend and act as you perceive a non-stressful person would act. Then recreate that action for yourself by acting or pretending, and guess what? You will become that stress-free person. Force yourself to change your thoughts. Force yourself to become an actor, to become an achiever.

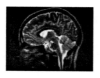

Brain Apples Implant #90: *Say it isn't so, Joe!*

A startling discovery originated in research at the University of California Irvine by Doctor Larry Cahill. We have had some discussions previously about research he was doing relative to emotions and memory and learning. He is a neuroscience expert in that area. Some of the research he is working on indicates that the brains of men and women are different and so they react differently. Those differences must be paid attention to for the achievement results you wish to attain.

For example:

1. The corpus callosum in women is larger, thicker and more involved with neuron connections than in the male corpus callosum. (The corpus callosum is that area of the brain that connects the left brain with the right brain.) Females are a bit more capable of using both sides of their brain in a coordinated fashion to come to conclusions and solutions to problems.

2. Dr. Cahill's research indicates that short-term stress can benefit learning in men, but inhibit it in females. So small amounts of stress act as an artificial emotion," but the triggering should be used differently by men and women!

Brain Apples Implant #91: Focus!

One of the things the brain scientists at Salk Institute have discovered relates to the ability to store and recall information in your long-term memory.

The brain can focus for only about 20 minutes at a time. That's it. And short-term memory lasts only about 45 seconds. So you have to take a break every 20 minutes when you are learning something new. But here comes the big one, the bad news one -- the important discovery.

Learning a new skill to coordinate all the neuron pattern inputs usually takes about 8 weeks. The brain must consolidate and organize your memories of a new task so you can perform that task at the highest level. Doggone it! There goes that quick fix again! No instant gratification. Success and achievement at the highest level take a lot of time and a lot of effort.

That doesn't even bother me anymore because I know, and now you know, that you can't possibly fail if you practice based on scientific principles. Of course, this scientific proof is not good news for those instant-gratification people who want their achievement levels to skyrocket overnight and who want to change their life in 15 minutes. But for those of us who learn this science and know that it will not fail, it is exciting news indeed!

Get over that instant gratification stuff! You want true success and achievement! It's not going to happen overnight. It's not going to happen in a week. Or 2 weeks. It takes 4 weeks to change your brain, and it takes at least 8 weeks to get to your highest level of achievement skills.

Whatever you do, *do not* tell any of this to your competition, because 90% of them will quit! 80% of them will quit before they even get to four weeks, let alone to eight weeks. Keep this information for yourself, your children, your students, your employees and those you care about and love. Take your achievements to the top of the mountain! I'll meet you there!

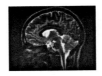

Brain Apples Implant #92: Sleep helps memory recall!

Remember we were talking about the 8 weeks it takes to get to the height of consolidation and coordination in your brain cells with new achievement skills? As you are learning new things, the hippocampus of the brain fills up in about 20 minutes, and then it needs a little time to consolidate that information and distribute it to the proper parts of the brain for memory storage. So, as we said, you should study in 20-minute spurts.

Sleeping also allows your brain to shore up memories of your learning, the places you visited, and the experiences you had in your previous waking hours so that sleep literally aids learning and memory, not the opposite, which has been a myth for a long time. I used to think that the reason students have to pull all-nighters to learn things was that, if they went to sleep, they would forget. In reality, sleep aids memory.

In research conducted by neuroscientists at the University of Liege in Belgium, it is clearly shown that, during sleep, there is increased and pronounced brain activity. This time-out leads to superior recall the next day and thereafter of memories created the day before that sleep. It just doesn't happen without the sleep. Use sleep to help you gain greater achievements.

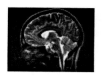

Brain Apples Implant #93: An apple a day keeps the doctor away!

Boy, that's an old expression, isn't it? Guess what? There may be some truth to it! Cornell University in Ithaca, New York, conducted a study on fruit and the brain and concluded that eating an apple every day keeps the Alzheimer's doctor away. There is a very strong antioxidant called quercetin in red apples (as well as in blueberries and cranberries) that fights cell damage in the brain—the damage caused by chemicals known as free radicals. Free radicals are generated by sunlight, chemical reactions and, guess what else? Stress! And this new study indicates that you can reduce your risk of developing Alzheimer's and similar brain-degeneration diseases by eating an apple a day. Let's go for it!

Eat an apple a day! AND **read a *Brain Apple* a day**! Why? Because if you do: *A*chievements, *P*roductivity, and *Performance* *L*evels *E*levate *S*ubstantially!

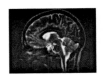

Brain Apples Implant #94: Brain Power is Unlimited! Bad news?

This is the least positive science lesson I'll share with you. Yet, it may also be the *most* positive science lesson I'll share with you. Here it is. The power of your brain, has no limit and can be used for *any* purpose.

I just came across some studies that make me reflect on the scientific knowledge that has been coming forth in the last 10 years that clearly indicates that if you learn about the workings of the human brain and procedures, techniques and skills based on that knowledge, **you have unlimited power for achievement.** That is the most positive discovery about the brain I've ever read!

But this power can also be negative. For example, UCLA did some research about the use of brain-imaging equipment and using the knowledge of brain functioning to influence, for example, the buying habits of Coke instead of Pepsi and influencing voters through advertising.

We make umpteen decisions at a non-conscious level. We have now gone through 93 lessons that clearly indicate that your brain makes some decisions in the non-conscious portions. Many times, people make decisions and don't even know why. Now here comes research indicating that people can be influenced without knowing it. During the last Presidential election, the influence of non-conscious impulse recognition and voters' decisions was studied by monitoring MRIs of Republicans and Democrats as they watched advertisements for each of the candidates. That is a frightening situation, isn't it? On one hand, it's scary to think that the advertising/political media would attempt to subconsciously influence our purchasing/voting decisions.

On the other hand, the positive implications of this research is there is now becoming a fast and universal belief that the power of the brain is unlimited for you and me to use for positive good and positive achievements, rather than negative.

I read another study from the University of California Irvine, unrelated to politics or purchase of Coke or Pepsi, about influencing non-conscious decisions in your brain to help you control your weight. You know we are certainly influenced non-consciously. My wife has mentioned to me at times that she doesn't like this food or that food because it relates to a past bad experience or a bad memory.

The study I was reading asked whether we could generate false memories associated with certain foods that cause us to gain weight, such as hamburgers, French fries and pizza. What if we could plant a false memory that indicates that a particular food is related to something bad in our past? Then we would stay away from that food. Tremendously powerful isn't it? Could even help children like broccoli!

The power of the brain is nearly unlimited, even to the point that understanding how the brain works can allow you to create false memories. We have seen in court cases where children were allegedly abused at a daycare yet they were, in fact, not abused. Somehow false memories had been planted in their brains. And, because of the repeated attention and focus paid to the allegations, they became real for those children. You can use your brain to achieve anything. **Ignore the negative; go for the positive.**

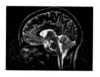

Brain Apples Implant #95: What is success?

I mentioned in Implant #10 that I was contacted by a well-known author to express what I felt were the secrets to success. That was a difficult question to answer. An even more difficult question is: What *is* success? I have told you that successful people are those who are constantly trying new things that they aren't even sure they know how to do. Successful people are those who look to see what everyone else is doing and choose, most likely, to do something else. But what is success itself?

Here is my definition of success. **To me, success is a feeling of forward motion—not arriving, but moving forward.** It is the journey, the feeling of mobility. It is the journey that counts, not the arrival.

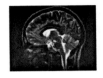

Brain Apples Implant #96: Get a personal coach.

Scientists have shown that, when you are praised and given encouragement, neurotransmitters and hormones are released in your brain. Those hormones, including endorphins and dopamine, give you a feeling of pleasure. They reduce the firing of pain impulses and increase the feelings of pleasure. If you have someone coaching you, someone you can talk to about your goals and the steps you are taking to achieve more, and that person encourages you, **your brain generates feelings of pleasure** that you will physiologically become addicted to and want to have return in your life. In other words, it will enhance your achievement levels.

Ironically, it doesn't matter whether that person is being honest with you or overemphasizing your abilities, skills and achievements. Your brain will respond as if what they are saying is real and will aid you in your achievements.

In fact, some studies indicate that people with a personal coach, achieved 20-25% percent greater accomplishments in the same amount of time as those who did not have a personal coach. You know from past lessons that the difference between a champion and an "also ran" is only 3-5% in performance levels and practice levels. So a personal coach can really benefit you!

Soon after I ran the Disney Marathon, I was sitting at a bar with a close woman friend of mine. Across the bar was a very attractive woman who was smiling at me. I said to my female companion, "Do you know that lady across the bar?"

"Oh yeah, that is Nancy. She works where I work and she gets promoted a lot and I can't figure it out. She got promoted over me for a job she wasn't even qualified for. She's been promoted about 5 times and she ... I just don't understand it. I'm much more skilled and qualified than she is but she keeps getting the promotions."

While this is being whispered in my left ear, around the bar comes this same woman and sits down next to me on my right-hand side and says, "You're Doug Bench, aren't you?"

"Yes, I am."

"I've heard a lot about you."

Apparently she had heard some things about me from the lady friend sitting on my left, whom I thought must have smoke coming out of her ears just now, but I was afraid to look.

"You ran the Disney Marathon, didn't you?"

"Well, yes I did."

"Oh wow! That's a tremendous accomplishment. What was your time?"

"Four hours and three minutes."

"Oh, that's fantastic, Doug! Man, that's quite an accomplishment! You should really be proud of yourself. Have you ever run the marathon before?"

"No."

"Oh, Doug, that's terrific! I'm so proud of you! It's a pleasure to get a chance to talk to you." And she walks away.

I'm calling, "Come back! Come back!" But then I turn to my companion and she mumbles something under her breath. I thought for a few minutes and then asked her more about this woman. And do you know what she told me? Nancy had also run the Disney Marathon! She didn't mention that to me. "I'm going to go talk to her some more," I say.

"Oh no," said my friend, "We have to leave now."

I eventually found out that Nancy not only ran the Disney Marathon, but she had run several marathons. She finished the Disney Marathon some 40 minutes ahead of me! Yet, when she came up to speak to me, she didn't present any information about her own skills as a runner. She praised me. She made me feel fantastic, even though I knew when she was saying how proud she was of me that she didn't really mean it! She was just flirting and building me up. It didn't matter; it made me feel like a million dollars.

Then it hit me. I know why Nancy has been promoted. She is a tremendous coach. She encourages. She praises. She knows how to make others feel good about themselves. Whether it's real or not real doesn't matter.

The brain takes it in as if it is real and causes pleasure. No wonder she has been promoted so many times. She brings out the best in others by praising them.

Get a coach and watch your achievements skyrocket!

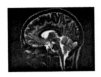

Brain Apples Implant #97: Become a personal coach.

You can benefit yourself by becoming a coach to someone else. It is scientifically proven that when someone coaches you, praises you and encourages you, positive neurotransmitters and hormones are released in your brain and you feel good and, therefore, will achieve more. Guess what? When you praise others, positive neurotransmitters are released in <u>your own</u> brain and you feel good about <u>yourself</u>. When you are confident about your actions and your position and your skills, your amygdala shuts up and you can expand your comfort zone. So not only get a personal coach, but be a personal coach to another and watch how that benefits them AND you!

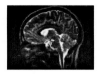

Brain Apples Implant #98: *Doug's Top Ten list.*

If I were stranded on a desert island, what ten books would I want to have with me? Here they are folks, my ten favorite books related to the science of advanced achievement, your brain, and your ability to reach the top.

1. ***Think and Grow Rich*** (Napoleon Hill), a classic book you must have. Written in 1939! 70 years ahead of its time!

2. ***The Magic of Thinking Big*** (David Schwartz). I include this book because it was the first book I ever read on the science of changing your life and personal development. It was not written from a scientific point of view. It, along with Napoleon Hill's book, is way too old to be scientifically based. But, man oh man, they are powerful! If you read those books keeping in mind what you have learned from this book about the science of your brain, you will see just how potent those two books are.

3. ***The New Brain*** (Dr. Richard Restak). His book contains (on Page 3) the most important quotation of the century relative to your personal development and achievements: "If you learn about the new brain research and learn techniques based upon the new brain research,

you can expect a lifetime of enhanced achievements."

4. **Mind Management** (Dennis Deaton). This book contains one of the top 3 secret powers for success ever!

5. **Change Your Brain, Change Your Life** (Daniel Amen). Chapter after chapter, I kept saying, "Yes! This brain science stuff really works!"

6. **A Celebration of Neurons** (Robert Sylvester). An educator extraordinaire. The title says it all.

7. **The Ultimate Guide to Mental Toughness** (Daniel Teitelbaum). A tough book to find and to read but you have to tough it out and find it and read it. Great exercises and science-based techniques

8. **The Eleventh Element** (Bob Scheinfeld). A little on the Spiritual side (rather than science-based), but well worth the trip.

9. **Learned Optimism** (Martin Seligman). You can learn to THINK like a winner.

10. **The Success Principles** (Jack Canfield). After interviewing over 100 success experts (including yours truly) Jack has determined the 64 principles of success. Read it and apply your brain science language to make it understandable and to make it more powerful!

11. Yes, there's a number 11, but it belongs on a separate list from the top ten. If you ever get lost or stranded or deserted, make sure you have a book that provides you personal strength and inspiration. That could be your Bible or it could be a book of poems written by your son. Whatever it is that brings you personal strength and inspiration, make that your 11th and most important book.

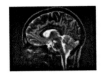

Brain Apples Implant #99: Take your daily vitamins.

What are your daily vitamins? Do these **10 things every day** for the rest of your life and you will get your daily dose of vitamins. From now on:

1. Any time anyone asks you how you're doing, the out-loud answer is a very positive, "I'm great! I'm terrific! I'm fantastic!" No matter how you really feel.

2. Commit to taking total, full responsibility for your circumstances, your results and how you feel. *Responsibility always trumps entitlement!*

3. Learn some new things every single day.

4. Stop yourself from completing any negative thought or statement that comes into your head and turn it into a positive-positive before you go on to anything else.

5. Do something new, strange, crazy, silly, out of the box or embarrassing—something that is otherwise not like you at all!

6. Set a goal by putting it down in writing. Write it down and make it happen.

7. Eagerly fail at something important and learn from it.

8. Tell at least two people that you love them; one of those must always be yourself even if you don't yet believe it.

9. Do an exercise regimen for your brain or body (preferably both).

10. Stop and see what everyone else is doing and then choose to go a different direction.

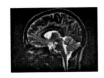

Brain Apples Implant #100. Take your REAL vitamins-everyday!

Taking vitamins every day not only helps your body, but also helps maintain your brain health. So do it every day and make sure you include pharmaceutical grade Omega 3 fish oil.

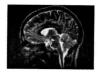

Brain Apples Implant #101: Scream!

Stand up and scream as loud as you possibly can...

"I am fantastic and I can achieve anything! I have tremendous brainpower! I can always advance my achievements!"

Hot damn! Hot dog! Yahoo!!

If you have read all 101 of these lessons, taken notes on them, implanted them in your brain and applied them all, your 'Do-it-Yourself' brain surgery has been a complete success!

You will soon be, or already are, one of the world's top achievers! Top 1%! Just turn on your motor and I will watch you go to the very top of the mountain!

Send me an email! Let me know how you're doing and how great the view is from there!

Doug Bench

For speaking engagements and media appearances,

or if you just want to chat, email me:

doug@brainapples.com